# SH*T
## ON MY
## HANDS

BY **BUNNY BANYAI**
AND **MADELEINE HAMILTON**

# CONTENTS

## 12–18 MONTHS

## 18–24 MONTHS

*Bunny dedicates this book to her firstborn daughter Clementine Louella Hall, and Tom, Beatrix and Peppa Carlyon, who in recent years have turned her life quite fantastically upside down.*

*Madeleine gratefully acknowledges
the breeding capabilities and support
of Michael Barrett,
who is a wonderful father
to Posy, Patience and Saul.*

# INTRODUCTION

There's very little to say about parenting that hasn't already been said a thousand times over, but given the breathtaking catalogue of manuals out there, the authors were surprised to find little material that really spoke to them when they became parents for the first time. Where was the filth, the fury, the mad love, the guru giving new parents a big metaphorical hug and whispering gently "you know, it's pretty hard to really bugger this up"?

The aim of this book is to cast no judgment, tell no lies, and soothe, rather than fray, the nerves of anxious first-time parents.

And remember – you've had house pets. You can do this.

# 0 – 6
## months

# BATHING

In the bad old days, freshly delivered babes went straight from birth canal to bathtub. We now know how important it is to keep them toasty warm and relaxed on mom or dad's bare chest, and also how valuable a few hours spent luxuriating in their own vernix is. So your newborn's first bath will likely occur once all that handy labor adrenalin has long departed and you're in the full throes of postnatal brain fatigue.

A hospital nurse will demonstrate the fine art of elevating baby's floppy head while gently sluicing his fragile skin. Endeavor as you might to pay attention, not even the prospect of drowning your newborn through incorrect hair-washing technique will keep you focussed. Instead, you'll be taking the opportunity while someone else is at the wheel to have a complete mental shutdown, or find yourself preoccupied with quandaries such as "How am I supposed to do that all-important post-birth crap with an arse that looks like a cross-stitch board?"

But very soon thereafter you'll be forced to use those baby-bathing skills … for while posing for the obligatory "here's baby about to enter his home for the first time" photographs on the front porch, said offspring will have the most monumental bowel explosion of his young life. It's at this point that you'll realize that while you have a drawer full of baby oils, lotions, balms, transcendental-meditation-for-tots CDs and a digital duck-shaped thermometer, you don't actually own a baby bath.

Which is why God invented sinks.

Fill the sink. Take a deep breath and, using a combination of common sense and the hospital instructions dredged from your subconscious, partially submerge your infant. Easy. "Actually, this isn't too bad. He seems to be enjoying it. (Well, he's not screaming, at least.) Ohhh, and I'm enjoying it too: it's so nice to caress my little one's skin while he stares in an endearingly catatonic manner at the pendant lights. I can talk to him about decoupage and he can't get away – in fact, he actually seems interested!"

Ah, yes. Bathing your baby at home for the first time will likely make you very happy you went through the reproductive caper, and, unlike the dachshund, he will find it difficult to roll about deliriously in a pile of manure once you've finished towelling him off.

# NAMES

Sooner or later you're going to want to give your newborn a name. It reduces the chance of any unfortunate nursery mix-ups, and gives people a reason to make fun of you. But unless you're completely bonkers (Hello, Sarah and Todd Palin! How's Track? And Bristol? And let's not forget little Trig!), the name game is tough.

There are many considerations for the thoughtful parent to take into account when naming their baby, including, but not restricted to, the following:

**1** *Should your kid be Emily no. 6 in her class, as a teen she may become the local meth cook in an effort to distinguish herself from her peers.*

**2** *You will invite the scorn and befuddlement of the world if you give her a traditional name, then disregard its regular spelling and cobble together a bunch of similar sounding letters to render it unique (Emmerlee).*

**3** *She may not appreciate being named after the village in which you and your partner lovingly fused sperm and egg. As an easily mortified* *adolescent this egregious and ever-present reminder of the fact that her parents actually did the deed – as well as precisely where in the world they did it – will not go down well.*

**4**  *It's great that you've found a brand of shin-guards that really go the distance on the soccer pitch, but that doesn't mean your progeny need be named after them (e.g., Tripp Easton Mitchell Johnston, Bristol Palin's son, named for his father's favorite brand of ice-hockey equipment). Similar restraint should be employed if you're contemplating a tribute to your favorite poodle-haired '80s rockers (e.g., Trig Van Palin, named for Van Halen).*

Aside from all of the above, remember that once your spawn starts walking you will be screeching her name roughly 3,000 times a day in an effort to prevent her decapitating herself and others. Long names will likely wind up shortened, if not by you then by everyone else. If the traditional shortening of your name of choice displeases you, a rethink might be in order.

Also, steel yourself for other people's reactions to your baby's name. Expect those who would normally be content to pass judgement behind your back to be gripped by a sudden attack of candor. Your family will likely wield the most blunt opinions. Father: "Clementine is a fucked name. You should call her Tina." Mother: "It sounds a bit

like the name of an antihistamine though, don't you think, darling?"
Grandma: "Oh, golly! That's what girls were called in my day.
Dear me."

Ultimately, though, you should disregard all the rules laid down by family, friends, guidebooks and us, and name your kid whatever you damn well please. Myxomatosis is a great name. Go on! Call her that!

## SWADDLING

Nurses are the true heroes of the maternity unit. Your doctor will visit for approximately half a microsecond, just enough time to make you feel fat, slovenly and intellectually inferior, before sweeping out of the room to scribble a bunch of indecipherable jargon into a manila folder for the nurses to try and decode. With all due respect to the wonderful, lifesaving stuff doctors do, it's the nurse who will do the grunt work.

Maternity nurses devote hours of study to the professional bondage of babies. Your nurse will wrap your baby tight enough to tie a string around and ship to Greenland. And though they'll show you the correct wrapping procedure ad nauseam, you will never, ever, come close to doing with a swaddling blanket what they can. You must accept this in the same way one accepts that one cannot administer morphine into their own buttocks …

## NURSING SCHOOLS HAVE A SPECIAL COURSE DEVOTED TO THE PROFESSIONAL BONDAGE OF BABIES

All wizened parents know that unless they have their own take-home nurse, they are doomed to make a mess of the swaddling routine every single time. Hence the thriving "wraps-for-idiots" market. We heartily endorse WFI, but finding the right one is like trying to select just one tooth to brush every night. Some have Velcro tabs. Some have zips. Some force the baby to sleep like they're the victims of a stick-'em-up robbery. Beg, borrow, steal or eBay some secondhand ones, and you'll soon work out, by their guttural howls or sweet snuffly snores, which one your baby likes best. Most babies do, puzzlingly, enjoy pretending to be a plastic-wrapped school sandwich, and are more likely to remain asleep during the lighter phases of their sleep cycle if they can't flail and squirm.

Hello, girls. No, not you. We're talking to your new tits. They are going to occupy a great swathe of your postnatal body, the parts usually reserved for your stomach, armpits and neck. We're not going to talk about whether you should or shouldn't breastfeed as we – in the nicest possible way – don't care. Judgement in all matters parenting related is unnecessary and unproductive. What you decide to do is a matter for you and your family – as long as you're not putting your baby in headbands with oversize bows. That's simply immoral.

When breastfeeding goes off without a hitch, it's quite an extraordinary thing. Note: "thing," not "achievement." If it doesn't work out, you haven't failed the first test of motherhood. "Not working out" includes simply deciding you don't much like it. It is an enormous physical undertaking that requires you to be on call 24/7, at least in the early months. Milk supply can also prove problematic – some women simply don't seem to produce enough to satiate their babies, while others produce so much that their lives become an endless merry-go-round of stuffing pads into bras, changing shirts and changing sheets.

Despite what you might read, breastfeeding will not prove the difference between your baby becoming Einstein or Hitler. You are no more or less of a woman or mother if you decide not to nurse. "Breast is best," goes the saying, but there's also that equally famous "happy mother, happy baby" creed. Do what makes you happy.

If you do decide to give breastfeeding a go, you need to know this: the arrival of the milk (around day three) will do things to your breasts you may have thought possible only with a plastic surgeon's intervention. It can also be quite painful. Imagine a truck full of cement being funnelled into your breasts, and then the truck catching fire.

This discomfort usually passes within a couple of days; in the meantime don't be too proud to pop the pills the nurses offer. You have hosted a human being for nine months in a space where you normally put toast, juice and muffins, so you've earned the right to a little comfort. Make sure all of the clothes you bring to the hospital provide for easy access to your nipples – tits twisted between layers of neck-high jersey will frustrate you and your baby to high hell.

Once your milk supply has established itself, you'll be able to start expressing milk so that your partner, family and friends can all have a go at feeding the baby. Watching a nursing mother pumping milk from her breasts via a machine that is a precise replica of industrial dairy machinery is truly a sight to behold. It's also one of the most powerful passion killers known to man, so one's breast pump should ideally reside at a discreet distance from the marital bed.

# EARLY FATHERHOOD

If you are the kind of guy who has a secret stash of *House Beautiful* magazines under the bed and prefers crocheting toy owls while watching reruns of *Frasier* to chugging beers at your local bar, then it might be quite empowering to discover that you do indeed produce sperm – robust, rudely healthy little swimmers of the successful egg-hunting kind. Unfortunately this feeling is likely to rapidly dissipate as you witness your female gestational carrier/dearly beloved deliver the final product – be she lying on an operating table having her internal organs rearranged, or howling like a banshee in a delivery room.

The good news is that once the creature is birthed those "I am but a mere male" feelings will melt right away if you roll up your sleeves and get stuck straight in. Your partner will be struggling with some combination of busted vagina, freshly sliced abdomen and unwieldy breasts, so anything you can contribute is not only going to be of enormous assistance, but will set the tone nicely for a future of shared parenting. Who needs a slew of scientific studies to know that closer parent–child relationships are enjoyed by fathers who take an active role from Day One?

Bathing, bottle feeds and, most significantly, bowel emissions can be your domain. Think of this as the next logical step in your evolution from toilet-humor-obsessed preteen to well-rounded, "Dad-joke"-cracking dude. Diaper changing provides much grist for the humor mill. Indeed, the only way to reconcile yourself to shit on your shirt is the knowledge that you will be able to tell this story to appalled friends and acquaintances for the rest of your life.

Hopefully you'll get a good chunk of time off work following baby's arrival, but sadly paid leave for non-primary carers is still considered by most employers as a bit newfangled, so before the placenta is delivered you're likely to be back at the office dealing with irritatingly well-rested colleagues. You're going to be exhausted. You'll be thinking quite a bit about Guantanamo Bay and whether the U.S. employed newborns to break the spirit of detainees.

You're likely to feel deprived of time with your infant child, while your partner may envy the perceived freedoms of the workplace while she's forced to acquiesce to the every squeak, squall and nipple-finding mission of your baby. Accept that baby is likely to be drop-kicked into your arms as soon as you walk through the door, and try

0–6 MONtHS

to negotiate a system whereby you both have the opportunity for an hour or two "off" each day. Alternate nights of taking on junior from sunset to sunrise. Never in your relationship will carefully considered words and selective deafness be as paramount as in those first few months of parenthood.

## PINK

The birth of a baby girl may be accompanied by feelings of great pride and hopes for the sort of unbreakable mother–daughter bond shared by Sally Field and Julia Roberts in *Steel Magnolias*, but it's also likely to herald the arrival of so much pink paraphernalia it'll look like a flamingo has thrown up in your hospital room. Baby pink onesies. Candy pink swaddling blankets. Teeny-tiny watermelon velour sweatpants (internationally recognized symbol of trailer-trash heritage). Hot-pink T-shirts with the words "I've got daddy wrapped around my little finger!" emblazoned across the front.

Lest we be taken for classist snobs, make no mistake: posh people buy copious amounts of rancid pink shit, too – it's just made in France instead of China.

Most females outgrow the desire for every stitch on their body and item on their shelves to be bright pink around the age of five, so it can be a tad alarming, not to mention infantilizing, to find yourself inhabiting a room that looks like it's had an extreme makeover masterminded by Barbara Cartland. The thing to keep in mind before you get understandably huffy about the fact that we still color-code babies according to gender, is that none of the people bearing garish pink gifts are trying to force your daughter into a rigid or regressive ideal of femininity. (Unless the gifts are being delivered by Jerry Falwell, or a rep from your local Toddlers and Tiaras pageant.) They're not trying to say "there'll be no Tonka trucks in your sandpit, young lady!" They're just trying to say "Congratulations!" in the most tried-and-true way of saying it – which is with pastel hues and helium.

Hopefully you'll have the chance to get your own back when the gift-givers' wedding registry requests Phillipe Starck "Louis Ghost" chairs and you hook them up with a plastic tits apron instead. Take comfort in this thought as you drink in your newly Barbie-fied surrounds and wipe baby drool from your shoulder with a pink stuffed unicorn.

# EXTREME PARENTING

According to some, it's not enough to simply love your baby, feed it when required and silently pray that it won't use up all your data allowance on porn when the first rush of hormones hits. You are also expected to align yourself with a particular parenting philosophy. And for some people, identifying themselves as being in one camp or the other is of vital importance. You've got the "attachment" advocates (demand feeding, co-sleeping, carrying baby in a sling rather than pushing him in a stroller); the "routine, routine, routine" crew (baby wakes at 6 a.m., bath at 6:15 a.m., play at 6:30 a.m., feed 6:45 a.m., if baby falls asleep during his feed place ice cubes in his ears, etc.); the "listen to your baby's cues" crew (Is the cry coming from his tummy or chest? Does he look like a constipated owl or a bewildered antelope when he cries? Does he tuck his legs into his chest or assume the downward dog position when he cries? All of the above, you say? Hmmm ... you need to listen more closely!); and finally the "emancipate your baby from the tyrannical grind of corporatized infancy" crew (no diapers, no rules and, clearly, no priceless Persian rugs).

There are sanatoriums filled with parents who tried to follow all the rules laid down by the baby tamers and whisperers. If your baby is one of the many who won't conform to the supposedly foolproof routines outlined by the self-appointed gurus, it doesn't mean you've not tried hard enough.

The overload of information can be counterproductive but perhaps even worse is the advice to "rely on your own instincts." Ah yes, instincts – those mystical, elusive vibes that will supposedly guide us through caring for our newborns. But as supremely difficult as it might seem, in time you can and will work out what suits you and your baby. Burn the damn guides and do what feels right. If that means baby falls asleep every night on the couch watching reruns of *The Golden Girls* with a heaving boob in his mouth for now, so be it.

## ECO-BABY

Every generation of mothers and fathers has to contend with some well-intentioned new child-rearing trend that will inevitably make them feel like a bucket of shit. Perhaps the biggest one of our time is the eco-baby movement. While the core idea – lessening baby's imprint on the planet and keeping her protected from toxic chemicals – is

0–6 months

undoubtedly sound, you can be left wracked with spasms of guilt for allowing a pesticide-laden strawberry to pass your child's lips. But hey, let's keep things in perspective. Giving your kid a chemically enhanced summer berry is hardly akin to putting bong-water in her bottle. Nobody ever lapsed into a coma after eating an apple purchased at a gas station.

There's also the indelicate matter of money. Glossy magazines smoothly advertise a dizzying array of trendy products with the whispered subtext "you are rubbish if you don't purchase this $2,000 handcrafted eco-friendly Scandinavian cot. Go ahead, buy that $100 Toys'R'Us number. Earth hater."

Don't beat yourself up because you can't afford the Scando-cage. Small, thoughtful, frequent gestures count more towards doing your bit than helping to prop up the huge not-always-cottage industry of ultra-luxe eco-everything. There are cheap, environmentally friendly cleaning products for baby and home available in most supermarkets, and buying a crocheted swaddling blanket from your local charity shop is just as ecologically sound as spending 90 bucks on an organic bamboo blanket. (And while it's true that organic bamboo blankets make you feel like you're being caressed by the satin-gloved hand of God, baby doesn't give a rat's ass – she's accustomed to living in a bloody mass of fluid and placental matter, remember.)

If, however, visions of an eco-friendly nursery stubbornly fill your fantasies, eBay does a thumping trade in secondhand baby goods. In fact, reusing and recycling other people's castoffs will earn you enough green points to justify a nice roll of deliciously smooth, bleached toilet paper, as well as disabuse you of the notion that having a baby is largely about buying a whole lot of bright, shiny, new stuff.

## STROLLERS

The acquisition of a stroller is only one of several necessary purchases likely to melt your brain prior to baby's arrival. But the amount of Internet research and surveying of friends you'll do before buying modern cloth diapers, a car seat or breast pump will be piddling compared to the energy you'll expend choosing what is essentially a glorified version of nana's shopping cart. Such is the bamboozling variety in strollers you'll contemplate strapping a harness and wagon to the labradoodle as the most straightforward option for transporting your offspring. But here are a few handy stroller purchasing tips should you not be in possession of a working dog:

**1** *If you'll be pushing the baby around on semi-rural unpaved roads, don't buy a stroller designed for the smooth, paved boulevards of Copenhagen. And if you haven't been running in a decade, you'd be foolish to start now, so step away from that ultra-fast and super-lightweight jogger.*

**2** *Test-drive before you buy. Spend hours in the local baby-goods emporium trying out every single model. The smallest idiosyncrasy in the suspension or steering will likely become a full-blown excuse to never take baby for a walk.*

**3** *Make sure the contraption isn't so heavy that it can't be lifted in and out of the trunk without causing a slipped disk, or so big that it won't fit through supermarket checkouts. And, fellows, please try not to use the purchase of a stroller as an excuse to demonstrate your masculinity: a hulking three-wheeler is not going to bolster your masculinity any more than a shiny red sports car. The stroller should not be viewed as a means of telling the world you have very large testicles. The same applies to ladies contemplating the purchase of a limited-edition Louis Vuitton Maclaren: there will only be tears (yours) when baby decides to try out a new spew/poo combo en route to the shops.*

Once you've laid out your hard-earned cash and brought home your new piece of baby transport, don't shove it in the corner next to the kitty litter box and tell yourself you'll figure it out once the baby's arrived. Practice folding and unfolding it, and make sure you know how to attach the sunshade, rain-cover and sippy-cup holder in record-breaking time. The last thing you want as a sleep-starved new parent is to be struggling to get the "FREAKING ASSHOLE OF A STROLLER" unfolded while junior screams in his car seat, the parking meter rapidly runs out, and the possibility of completely missing your very important appointment with the physical therapist/psychiatrist/sleep consultant becomes very real.

Be assured that in the above scenario no-one will come to your assistance. That is because strollers are universal objects of loathing. So pissed off is the average citizen with being slowed down by buggy-pushing parents on footpaths, at street crossings and in shopping malls, or with having their style cramped by the eternally un-hip contraptions in cafes, that they will merrily ignore your frantic wranglings. Such moments are high up in the Top Ten miseries of early parenthood.

But once you master the finer peculiarities of your stroller it will truly prove a godsend. Pushing it up and down hills will help keep you fit and healthy, as well as melt any unwanted pregnancy padding. If baby refuses to sleep in his crib or, indeed, anywhere in the house, he may blessedly conk out once moving (it's best that you actually accompany him on such trips, despite any temptation to let go of the contraption from the top of a steep incline and kick back for a curbside nap of your own). There is perhaps no greater joy than languorously strolling in the sweet air and sunshine, singing a Madonna medley to your much-amused baby, while studiously ignoring the huffing and irritated sighing of a mealy-mouthed suited type trying to pass by.

## CARRIERS

There are as many different kinds of carriers as there are shades of baby poo. You're likely to learn what's best for you through trial and error. See if you can try out a couple of your friends' carriers before you spend big bucks on a popular brand that then turns you into a crippled human banana, or requires a degree in structural engineering to operate. Be realistic about the circumstances in which you may actually use one:

impressed as you may be by the opportunities Carrier A provides for mountain-hiking with a six-month-old on your back, if you can't actually think of anything worse than all-terrain boots and sensible socks, let alone with a squawking infant in tow, then move right along.

Likewise, when friends rave about how great Carrier B was when they were traipsing across Europe, with its multiple pockets for passports, tickets and Orangina, you may want to check your bank balance before investing in the same. If you have barely enough money for plastic wrap – let alone international airfares – costly carriers that double as backpacks will be disappointingly underutilized.

**TRY OUT A COUPLE ... BEFORE YOU SPEND BIG BUCKS ON A POPULAR BRAND THAT THEN TURNS YOU INTO A CRIPPLED HUMAN BANANA**

You may even find you don't need one at all, and that a stroller does everything you require. But baby carriers do have some really super benefits: they let you hold your child close while leaving your arms free to wash dishes, weed the vegetable garden and send pictures of kittens to your BFF. And baby will love the proximity to you too. She can monitor your facial features and expressions (try not to get paranoid about this – she is learning about language and communication, not staring into your soul and concluding you have a heart of darkness), and the constant repetitive movements of mundane domestic tasks will soon lull her to sleep.

Above all, baby carriers give you greater mobility, and this is something in dreadfully short supply as soon as you take delivery of your newborn. Being able to strap her on and head to the shops on foot is about as liberating as things get once you become a parent. There are even some models that enable mothers to maneuver hungry, cranky babies onto a breast, allowing the novel sensation of having your nipple suckled while walking home from the bus stop.

## CRYING

A pox on you, Mother Nature: this was the most sophisticated way of allowing babies to communicate that you could think of? Really? Maybe after producing seahorses that could change color in order to evade predators, and pigs that can sniff out the most expensive fungus known to man, you were feeling slightly spent, even a little malicious, and determined that a crude yowling screech was all the vocabulary an infant human needed.

Fuck the baby whisperers. All crying babies sound the same – with minor variations in volume and frequency. If you can determine the difference between a "tired" cry, a "dirty diaper" cry or a "hungry" cry, then you should be employed by the Bureau of Meteorology to sit atop a mountain and predict catastrophic weather events. When they're first born, babies can lull you into a false sense of cautious relief. Often they're rather quiet for the first 48 hours. "He's perfect, he hardly even cries!" you crow to your friends. Best to take into account the following:

**1** *Your baby is exhausted from being born. Seriously. He squeezed himself through a vagina. Or recoiled in shock as a gloved hand entered his home and wrestled him out into a theater of poorly dressed clones in white masks. Can you imagine?*

**2** *There's a distinct possibility he's revelling in the same dreamy post-op bliss as his mother.*

A new parent can quite understandably decide the whole crying lark is nonsense and try to find a solution to it. Be warned: this is a Bad Place. This is the Road to Madness. Because in every pharmacy, every bookshop, every health-food store, every Internet forum, you will find six million wildly conflicting theories on How to Stop the Crying. Elevate baby's head. Take him to a chiropractor. Don't drink orange

0–6 MONTHS

**023**

juice. Chickpeas? You eat CHICKPEAS? OF COURSE he's crying: he's mainlining farty bean juice via your breast milk!

It's possible, of course, that the first thing you try in order to stop the crying will actually work. Or you may find something that works only after the 5,999,999 other options have been tried and failed. Much money and precious time can be sapped in this pursuit when what's really required is both a stiff drink and upper lip.

The crying phase passes before you know it. In rare instances it's unbearable and prolonged and medical advice should be sought, but the majority of babies do just cry, and it's not because they have constipation or reflux or deep psychic pain. Don't take it as any kind of great personal failing on your part OR baby's if he screams for a few hours every night. Partake in whatever personal indulgence or vice you need to get through it, and don't be fooled by those at your parents' group who say their baby doesn't cry. If you fess up to having an infant who does, indeed, cry, you'll find a bunch of grateful, hollow-eyed zombies sidling up to you and conceding that "actually, Ja Rule has had a difficult night or two." Crying is normal. Blame Mother Nature for not giving you an infant who changes color according to his needs.

# SLEEP – PART ONE

Newborn babies have great reputations when it comes to being uncorrupted, smooth-skinned and adorable. Where sleep is concerned, their reputations fare less favorably. Without wanting to harp on relentlessly about the failures of Mother Nature, this, along with crying, earns her another pox. Sleep deprivation psychosis, as far as your authors can see, never helped anyone. Unless you're Margaret Thatcher, you're unlikely to exclaim "I had two hours sleep last night and it's done me a power of good!"

The number of hours per night that their baby sleeps brings out a strangely competitive streak in some parents. On one side you have the people who boast that from Day One their sweetie has woken but once a night, alerting her parents to the fact with nothing more offensive than a limp whimper, before settling easily back to sleep with a quick pat to the back. The flip side is those who compete to be the most exhausted by sleep deprivation: "My baby woke every hour-and-a-half last night." "Oh, is that right? You're lucky. I'd be fine with that. My baby woke every half-hour." "Well, my baby woke every 15 minutes. And she vomited all over her sheets. Then her head spun round and round in wild jerking motions while she projectile vomited irradiated-green liquid and growled 'badmommybadmommybadmommy'".

It's advisable, when listening to these stories, to remember that your fellow new parents are just as out of their minds as you are.

If baby doesn't sleep through the night at an early age, don't feel pressured to implement the routines espoused by the army of baby-sleep gurus. They will assure you at length that your infant KNOWS how to sleep through the night, and it's YOUR meddling ways that have prevented her from doing so. If you just stick to THIS particular routine with ABSOLUTELY NO VARIATIONS, your ten-day-old will sleep through the night. And lovingly tend to your bonsai collection.

This is bonkers. Your baby wakes up because her stomach's the size of an ant's penis and she needs regular feeding. She's also adjusting to living in a house constructed of bricks and mortar rather than organs and fluid. Also, don't forget that about the only form of entertainment she can produce for herself is the trick of going to sleep and waking up. Little wonder she will play around with endless variations on the theme.

And remember, every time a two-week-old sleeps through the night, God kills a kitten.

# PACIFIERS

Before you have a baby you may have high-minded thoughts like "No child of mine will ever use a pacifier" and "People who give pacifiers to kids are clearly lazy or incompetent". But after a month of haplessly trying to settle your fractious newborn, you'll likely be yelling at your partner, or the wall-mounted singing fish, "Where's the goddamn pacifier? QUICK! Screw it, just pass me that tennis ball, that'll do!" After some initial trepidation about any object that's not a warm and friendly mama's nipple or a top-of-the-line BPA-free bottle passing junior's lips, you'll be happily reaching for the pacifier as an avenue of first resort – especially if it actually works.

Maddeningly, some babies just don't take to pacifiers, preferring to exercise their right to scream unplugged, but if yours accepts one, sucks contentedly until he falls asleep, then remains shut-eyed from dusk till dawn, you'll be hastily revising your ideas about the ill effects of substitute nipples. Babies like to suck. A lot. They're like tiny human pool filters. If you don't want your index finger or nipples to become your baby's primary source of comfort, consider the pacifier an essential accessory.

But like peach schnapps, French cheeses and Mike and the Mechanics records, too much of a good thing can lead to habituation and negative physical effects. Binging on booze and rich food mean a pickled liver and huge backside for you, Mike and the Mechanics' musical stylings have similar effects on your brain as Mad Cow disease, and a prolonged (post 24 months) affair with a pacifying glob of plastic equates to possible compromised speech development and wonky teeth for baby.

There's also the vexed issue of preschoolers who won't relinquish their pacifiers except when sleeping. So at some stage you're going to have to put away your little silicone friend and find another way – unless, of course, you want to be the parent of a buck-toothed 40-year-old with a vocabulary of five words and an oral fixation that renders him a social pariah ("Oh darling, we can't invite Trevor to the party. He sucks his shirt collar. And his bail conditions won't allow it. Tell me, did that wretched mother of his allow him a pacifier past early infancy?")

# SOOTHING

If you're one of the many mad cat people of this world then you'll know that when your feline is unsettled you put her on your chest, stroke her head and say nice things about her fangs. You may not see any reason why this approach wouldn't work with a baby, too. And yes, you're absolutely right! Soothing pets and babies really isn't so different. Cats can wail at a frequency just as ear-shattering as any newborn's. They can keep it up all night, just like a newborn. And often there's no telling precisely what it is that's disturbed their delicate equilibrium. Just. Like. A. Newborn.

So, if you're thinking that you might actually be quite well equipped for parenthood because you've been the proud but tired owner of a particularly precious pet, you're probably not too far off the mark. But you're well advised to keep these thoughts under your hat. "Ridicule the Deluded Expectant Parent Who Thinks They're Prepared" is a game many old-timers like to play ("nothing can prepare you" they trill, voices dripping with a curious mix of saccharin and bleach). Implying that a pet who routinely takes up residence in a linen cupboard for 48 hours has prepared you for parenthood will have them merrily declaring you in need of psychiatric evaluation.

Clearly, they've never owned a pedigree puss.

# SEX FOR MOM

In the weeks following your child's arrival, the prospect of sex probably seems as likely as your joining a two-week horseriding expedition or winning a gold medal for figure skating at the Winter Olympics. Parts of you will be feeling very fragile indeed, and just the thought of someone rubbing them (however worshipfully) will make you want to hail a taxi to the local convent. However, while engorged breasts, leftover pregnancy hemorrhoids and the close proximity of a bleating infant don't usually arouse lust for anything but unbroken sleep, some women want to get back into the bedroom as soon as possible, hungry for sex that isn't restricted to the approximately two positions one is capable of performing in the last trimester of pregnancy.

Even once the mandatory six weeks of crossed legs and wasted erections post-birth period have passed, many women still only want to remove their underpants while on the toilet or in the shower. But after nearly two months of being a complete slave to your newborn, you might start thinking it would be nice if someone whispered a few sweet somethings into your ear. Now you could slip into your long-neglected fishnet stockings and Tangerine Dream lipstick, perch on a bar stool and accept expensive cocktails and sexy platitudes from strange men with ridiculous facial hair, but for the sake of your new little family it's probably advisable to try a little intimate talk and snuggle time with your partner first.

Don't rush things if you're not yet physically or mentally comfortable with the concept (the mere mention of sex may well have you drawing your knees together and turning the page). You'll know it's time to attempt sex when the post-birth amnesia has fully kicked in and you can again conceive of your private parts as an amusement park rather than the setting of a horror film.

## VACCINATIONS

Just as dog kennels will refuse to board your canine without a meticulous vaccination schedule signed and stamped by your vet, childcare providers may exclude non-immunized children if there's an outbreak of a vaccine-preventable disease. Unlike dogs though, children can't spend the hours you're at work in the backyard rummaging with their snouts for long-buried bones and barking at the wind, so complying with your childcare provider's terms and conditions is well-advised.

Few parents will be oblivious to the controversy that's swirled around certain vaccines of late, and even if you sensibly decide that it's better to immunize than not, it can be quite a hand-wringing experience watching said vaccine slide into baby's chubby little arm. If you feel inclined to do some research on the topic, avoid Internet musings – they range from the passionately pro- to the fervently anti-vaccine, and the effect on you is likely to be abject confusion. Instead, go to a doctor you trust for balanced and evidence-based information. They're a far more reliable source of information than AngelsBreath211 or Pantsonfire35.

If you're still feeling fretful about any pain or distress the jab will cause (baby, not you), rest assured it will be short-lived and dissipate entirely when the nurse proffers a balloon stamped with a giant pharmaceutical logo.

## FIRST OFFICIAL "DO"

Many new parents decide to celebrate the arrival of their offspring by throwing a party for family and friends. The backyard gets dolled up with bunting, and a table full of soft cheeses, salami and shellfish laid out as a mark of respect to the mama who endured nine months of pointed sideways glances from strangers every time she so much as blinked at a block of gorgonzola.

If you're not religiously inclined, such events are a good way of showcasing your baby and bagging a new round of bibs and onesies. But even the staunchly agnostic amongst us can feel somewhat cheated at the end of the day. After all, you have successfully survived the first months of parenthood, and you have an infant who would look majestic in a flowing white gown. The backyard is a perfect spot for emptying kegs and barbecuing sausages till they look like petrified dog poo, but it's somewhat lacking in pomp and ceremony. Where are the stern-faced men invested with celestial authority, the soaring songs of praise, the mysterious water-torture rituals/foreskin removals?

**WHERE ARE THE STERN-FACED MEN INVESTED WITH CELESTIAL AUTHORITY, THE SOARING SONGS OF PRAISE, THE MYSTERIOUS WATER-TORTURE RITUALS/ FORESKIN REMOVALS?**

Your older relatives will doubtless weep with gratitude if you go down this route. Your younger relatives will be compelled to don suits that comprise of more than just a T-shirt with a tux print. Your crazy Uncle will be obliged to keep his feelings about women being permitted to vote under his hat. And, admit it: deep down, part of you craves the opportunity to don a politely flirty dress-and-hat combination à la Princess Kate, does it not?

Life is generally an unceremonious affair. We could all do with a little more ceremony, frankly. Many couples get married not because they are hot for a lifetime of monogamy, more because they want to have a nice big party but can't think of a theme to top that one where everyone had to come dressed as their favorite gardening tool. Grand social occasions are few and far between post-baby. This is your opportunity. Seize the day!

## PRIMAL INSTINCTS

Homicidal urges aren't generally regarded as something evolved adult human beings should expect to experience regularly. The birth of a child can, however, release previously untapped killer instincts in even the gentlest beacons of pastel Christian winsomeness among us. A new parent pushing a two-week-old down the street might look benign, but the merest hint of a threat to their tiny infant will have them swiftly reaching for the bayonet under the Bugaboo.

The protective ferocity of a freshly minted mother or father is truly a wonder to behold. They will nod sagely at tales of mother bears mauling

hapless trespassers, and by way of sympathy say: "Well, they shouldn't have gone for a hike in that neck of the woods now, should they?"
A short car trip is accompanied not by the usual thoughts of "Do I need gas/What's wrong with pop music today?" but sentiments such as "If I see a driver engaged in an act of road thuggery that could endanger my swaddled newborn, I will sew their feet to their backside."

Newborns are vulnerable little packages – few people are unmoved by the sight of their helplessness and they inspire feelings of great tenderness and devotion in those who had a hand bringing them into the world. Those feelings are wonderful, but they aren't going to protect the baby from predatory animals and situations unless accompanied by some grittier, grizzly-bear-like instincts. It's nevertheless unnerving for those of us who've spent our adult lives deploring acts of violence and eating tofurkey at Christmas to suddenly be occupying the headspace of a trigger-happy vigilante.

The initial intensity of these feelings will eventually mellow into something slightly less rabid, leading you to realign yourself with your old pacifist ideals and peel the "I Shoot and I Vote" bumper sticker off the car.

# ADJUSTING TO A NEW LIFE

Some time after delivering your baby – possibly even before returning home from the hospital, heavy with the knowledge that the morphine drip can't come with you – the blues might strike. It's small comfort to know that most women experience this in some form or another, whether it's Day Three Blues or a wave that rolls in much later and lasts much longer. Having a baby may be one of life's most universal experiences, but that doesn't mean it can't also be an isolating one.

In addition to tending to the sometimes bedevillingly complex needs of a newborn, and coping with wildly fluctuating post-pregnancy hormones, the loss of your pre-baby life is a major contributor to distressing postpartum feelings. Doctors can offer you referrals to a bunch of excellent services for women with postpartum depression; we can offer what we hope are helpful pointers on how to feel better about your new state of affairs.

1   *Resist the temptation to cut yourself off from your friends and wallow with only your heaving bosom and jaundiced newborn for company. Just because you've had a baby doesn't mean you've*

*amputated the part of yourself your friends love. (Unless they love
you because of a shared interest in sex orgies. Then the friendship
might, indeed, be compromised.) They won't think you're a bore just
because you have to watch* Mad Men *with baby in your lap instead
of holding their hair back while they vomit and blather incoherently
about how they could really inject some INTELLECTUAL CLOUT
AND RIGOR into the* Big Brother *house. Your old routines may have
been turned on their heads and your bedtime wound back three
hours, but you haven't had a personality bypass. If you can remind
yourself of this, your friends will inevitably agree.*

**2**   *Realize that your professional identity, which has perhaps defined
you since the end of high school, is only on temporary hiatus.
Yes, it's true that for at least a little while you're not a teacher,
journalist or IT whiz, but rather a collection of body parts dedicated
to the continuing growth and well-being of a tiny human. Despite
the glee you felt when embarking on maternity leave, between
changing diapers and sterilizing bottles you might be surprised
to find yourself emailing Debbie in Sales to check in on things.
The most senior members of society speak the honest truth when
they say "It all goes by so fast" – meaning your baby will be fully
grown and on a hallucinogenically assisted backpacking trip across
the Subcontinent before you know it. Best to indulge yourself in*

0–6 MONtHS

*admiring his every infantile squeak and wiggle now, rather than waste your time worrying about whether a brainless 20-year-old is trying to take over your turf, or, more alarmingly, whether Ian in customer service has filched your stapler.*

**3** *If you have a partner, try to stay confident that the changed dynamic between the two of you will not equate to a long-term disaster. You may have thought the miracle of new life had permanently cemented your bond, yet in the following weeks you'll be staring daggers at your partner as they snore luxuriantly while you hoist your tits out for the umpteenth feed of the night. The necessity of taking shifts to care for the colicky newborn, sleeping in different rooms, and the baby's ability to dominate not only the physical space between the two of you but also all your conversations, can make you yearn for those pre-baby days when you had unpressured discussions about architectural design, and only mutual friskiness and early morning garbage trucks disturbed your sleep. While it's true the freedom and spontaneity of those days can't really be recaptured, your relationship can evolve into something else entirely that might prove to be even more satisfying than the old days of unfettered lovemaking and luxuriant sleeping.*

**4** *Going to fancy restaurants and the theater or cycling down Icelandic glaciers might be off the cards for now, but you will likely fill the void with Facebook and Instagram. And that's ok. You've had a baby.*

*They are lousy dinner dates, they don't care for Broadway shows, and you are not even allowed to take them on a plane until they are at least two weeks old. So you deserve a free pass to binge on social media. But do keep yourself in check – you do not want to alienate your childless friends (there is always that one person on your Instagram feed who shares regular posts of baby's every fart and digestive rumblings). A good rule of thumb is that every baby-related post should be followed by three consecutive non-baby posts – and you will be delighted to hear that cat photos are fine and do not count toward your baby-photo allowance …*

# 6 – 12
## MONTHS

# ALLERGENS AND DIRT

In the past decade, scientific studies have revealed the health benefits of small amounts of red wine and dark chocolate. Yet pregnant women generally avoid these two "medicines" (thank tabloid photos of sad-eyed fetal-alcohol-syndrome babies and the crushingly unfair link between rampant heartburn and any cocoa-based product for that one). Indeed, the majority of pregnancy-related studies have absolutely no benefit to knocked-up chicks except to make them worry that one accidental nibble of feta or split second of kitty-litter contact will consign their offspring to a lifetime of woe.

But there is some university-based research that actually works in the new parent-to-be's favor. For example, there's a strong and proven link between overly clean houses and the rise of food allergies and asthma in the affluent, germophobic West. Too much hospital-grade shower cleaner = underdeveloped kiddie immune systems. Overzealous dustbusting of cat hair may actually harm your unborn child more than smoking a cigarette or drinking a beer*.

This is exactly the kind of news you want to hear when your pregnant girth precludes operating the vacuum cleaner. And when Aunt Myrtle, whose bleach obsession extends to floor surfaces yet not her mustache,

*Though probably not.

suggests the employment of a professional cleaner to deal with all the ghastly bacteria and debris your home is harboring, you can, with science on your side, tell her you're protecting the health of your unborn (or, alternatively, say "I don't give a flying fuck about my floors, Myrtle"). Hooray!

But even as you continue this non-cleaning regime long past baby's arrival, scrubbing the toilet only when people begin to compliment you on the tasteful shade of chocolate brown you chose for the commode, there's a bit of Aunt Myrtle that stubbornly resides within you. Try as you might to abandon all that cultural conditioning about germs and dirt, a reflex response will have you jumping out of your chair when your baby gleefully reclaims the banana slice off the floor and stuffs it in her mouth.

And it's not just your own reactions that will have you lingering in the supermarket household cleaning products aisle. Comments like "Oooh, look at those dirty little fingernails!" and "How lovely that you're relaxed enough as a parent to let her eat compost" will inevitably have you scrubbing, sweeping, mopping and filling the baby bath like June Cleaver on crystal meth.

Just as your house-cleaning tendencies will stubbornly lurk, so too will you feel innate parental trepidation when introducing your baby to any new food that might, just might, induce throat swelling or hives. If you have a severe case of anaphylaxis anxiety, park outside a hospital when giving the little one her first peanut-butter sandwich or boiled egg.

Despite your best efforts, your offspring will inevitably come into contact with something that will cause an allergic reaction – especially during her oral fixation stage when any inanimate object or insect scuttling past is deemed worthy of immediate tongue exploration. Be aware that she may misinterpret *The Very Hungry Caterpillar* as The Very Hungry Baby That Ate a Caterpiller, and consequently have a nasty encounter with the acid-spitting real thing in the backyard. Likewise, your politely disinterested praise of your neighbor's rhododendrons may be taken as an invitation to lick them.

Hopefully when you catch the suppressed grin of the emergency room nurse as you breathlessly explain the reason your ten-month-old has a mouth the size and color of a baboon's ass, you'll see the amusing side of your darling's oral explorations and not take such episodes as a damning indictment of your parenting skills. And when Aunt Myrtle reacts with horror to news of this incident, you might remind her that she has a permanent caterpillar residing on her top lip.

# BREASTS/WEANING

We all know the benefits of breastfeeding, but for many women continued breastfeeding is preferable to formula simply because sterilizing bottles is a royal pain in the ass. However, even if you intend to keep feeding until your child has constructed their first solar system project, circumstances may intervene. Due to illness or suddenly acquired employment, you might find yourself undertaking a rapid wean far earlier than planned.

As doctors now prefer not to prescribe medication to dry up milk supply, you'll likely be doing it the natural way – which is akin to running a marathon with turtles strapped to your feet. Your breasts will initially be engorged and lumpy, and you'll be bellowing like an unmilked cow. Cabbage leaves, hot showers and over-the-counter painkillers provide scant relief. Your baby's every grumble and giggle will prompt your breasts to reload with milk, and sleep will be fitful due to the burning hot agony of the rumbling twin volcanoes on your chest.

Sudden weaning, needless to say, should be avoided as strenuously as dinner invitations from Breatharians.

Be aware that when the milk goes, your breasts will undergo yet another rapid transformation. If you've spent the nursing period with breasts so large they're virtually a country unto themselves, singing their own national anthem and waving little flags, you may be shocked to note they're now no more than glorified skin tags, swaying about forlornly in a woefully oversize bra.

What you need in this instance is not a trip to Thailand for a cut-price boob job, but an old-school department store bra fitter called Maureen. She may be 95 years old and look like a crushed cigarette, but she'll swiftly maneuver your shopworn tits into a killer bra that creates the illusion of shape and form.

# GENITALS

Despite the prevalence of genitalia in every kind of digital and traditional media, ours remains a repressed society when it comes to frank discussions about sex and descriptions of said organs. Just as teenagers blanch at the mere thought of their parents ever having sex, from the day your baby is born you too will seek to remain willfully ignorant of the reproductive purpose of your child's genitals.

As far as you know – and would happily continue to believe forever – that is just what they pee out of.

As your child grows, however, you can't escape the fact that she will become interested in her genitals. Each gender may express this curiosity differently but babies of both sexes often have a bit of a public fiddle.

Religious schooling, wacky parents, paranoia about the aesthetic appeal of your own private parts and bad sexual experiences may have left you with hang-ups about genitalia generally, but for your own kids' sake try to discuss genitals in a way that doesn't make them feel embarrassed and lead to a life of shameful fumblings and lights-off-only lovemaking or, alternatively, an "Up yours, mom and dad!" career in porn. Try:

**1** *Rethinking your use of any cutesy terminology: "fifi", "tootie" and "pee pee" are great names for guinea pigs but they infantilize both parent and child and lack the straightforward precision of correct anatomical terms.*

**2** *Not to break down into hysterical laughter (or tears) when your darling engages in some kind of Puppetry of the Penis/Vaudeville of the Vagina performance art at grandma's retirement afternoon tea for Father Gerald. It will only make them connect strong emotion with ordinary body parts.*

**3** *Closing your ears to any advice you may receive about restraining your child's self-exploration. It may have been common in years gone by to sew up the pockets of boys' pants so they couldn't manhandle their members, but tuberculosis and backyard abortions were common then, too. Try to take a more enlightened approach: masturbation not only helps young ones develop confidence and familiarity with their own sexuality, but is a great way to pass time when there's a power failure. Just guide them towards the habit of private indulgence by discreetly nudging them towards the bedroom when their hands go past the waistband of their pants. However progressive you may be, public masturbation is never a good look.*

## GRANDPARENTS

It's a fair bet that when your mom and dad were babies they were tossed in a bassinet for car trips and given pacifiers dipped in honey. Grandparents are marvelous creatures in that they're generally as besotted by your child as you are, but they're not always well-versed in current child-rearing practices. Where you might see the silverware drawer as a cabinet packed with lethal weaponry, your father sees a drawer filled with fun old-fashioned playthings. Suggesting to him that a non-toxic rubber giraffe might be a better teething device than a bottle opener will be met with a loud guffaw and a bemused shake of the head: "How did anyone ever survive childhood back in our day, eh?" Indeed.

Attempting to shoehorn your parents into best-practice child-rearing methods is ill-advised, however tempting. Gen Xers resent embryonic hipsters parading about clad in the bustiers, cut-off denim shorts and lace-up boots that were all the rage c. 1991 – it's difficult to resist the urge to grab them by the scruff of their Stüssy T-shirt and start grumbling about having worn all this garbage the first time round. Your parents feel the same way about present day child rearing "experts". "We raised four kids without any gurus breathing down our necks about routines and death traps and you all survived." They have a point. It's nonetheless unnerving watching your mom whispering sweet nothings to the cat in the front yard while your ten-month-old lies happily in the dog's basket gnawing on a pig's ear treat.

Just try and think of the last time you read a news headline announcing: "Toddler Injured in Old-Fashioned Child-Rearing-Practice Incident, Grandmother Out on Bail." It's reassuringly infrequent.

# HEALTH PROFESSIONALS

Slapped cheek disease. Kawasaki disease. Epiglottitis. Coxsackie virus. Don't be fooled by their fun, wacky names: these illnesses have the power to send you hurtling headlong into the nearest fiery pit. Coping with sick, fretful babies is undoubtedly one of the most soul-sucking aspects of parenting. You'll seesaw between wanting to stroke their fevered brows and feeding them to the lions. But hateful viruses are to babyhood as supermodels are to Roxy Music video clips: you can't have one without the other.

What can make the whole experience more bearable are the ministrations of a competent and sympathetic doctor. Your own doctor may be fabulous at pap smears and diagnosing obscure STIs, but if she lacks a reassuringly confident and kind approach to baby's ailments and your resulting anxiety, shop around for one who doesn't. Interrogate every parent you know about where they go when their kids' snot or shit production ramps up to alarming levels. Ask these questions of any potential new doctor's office:

**1** *Does the toy box look as if it could be the source of a cholera outbreak?*

**2** *Does the staff actually like children and display some familiarity with their peculiar afflictions, or do they give the impression they wished they were still at med school with a scalpel and a cadaver?*

Should you be lucky enough to be directed to the world's best baby-friendly doctor, make sure you uphold your end of a civilized doctor–patient relationship. Clean up your child's various expulsions; refrain from exhibiting a bad temper even if you're slack-jawed with sleep deprivation; and, no matter how tempting that whole doctor–patient porn scenario is, don't EVER make a sexual pass. You might view them as the comely provider of comforting explanations and powerful prescriptions, and as the one who MADE THE BABY STOP CRYING. They view you as a person with chronic mouth ulcers who will happily pee in a cup if asked to. Thank them for their time and attention and pay your bill.

Respect their right to remain ignorant of your ailments outside of office hours. When you run into them sharing a margarita with their spouse at the local pizza joint, don't feel it necessary to get them up to speed on the state of your gallbladder.

Then there's the matter of what sort of medication or pain relief you'll allow baby to ingest. It's one thing to stuff all kinds of painkillers into your own mouth, but the issue of what passes baby's lips requires more careful consideration. Some parents won't allow anything other than herbal preparations to be given, except in the direst of emergencies. Others combine traditional and alternative therapies. And some are happy to put their faith in tried-and-true over-the-counter kiddy elixirs. Curiously, you'll find the friends who always took an impressively cavalier approach to their own drug use are often loathe to administer any kind of pharmaceutical relief to their children.

Many doctors have a service for after-hours home visits, which can be particularly valuable if you want to avoid the misery of hospital waiting rooms. But if things look seriously worrying, the local emergency room is the only place on earth you'll want to be.

## NAYSAYERS

On the day your child is born you will receive nothing but positive feedback. Not only is she a miracle and the most beautiful thing on earth, but you are extraordinary for having created her. The good times will keep rolling for some months to come – to be ordained a "good" mom seems a pretty straightforward business and goes something like this:

1. *Feed child with the milk that has created your eruptive bustline, or, if breasts are reticent performers, a trusted top-of-the-line formula.*

2. *Watch child turn from squinty-eyed, reptilian-looking critter into cherubic, wide-eyed darling.*

3. *Serenely accept all compliments concerning her bountiful thighs and squirrely red cheeks.*

4. *Don't fall asleep on top of her after imbibing an unmemorable amount of vodka.*

To be considered a "good" dad, simply:

1. *Pose for "tasteful" black-and-white portraits cradling the nude infant against your freshly waxed bare chest.*

2. *Read aloud excerpts from Keith Richards' bio until infant falls asleep in an understimulated stupor.*

**3** *Take the baby to the shops for milk and bread. (Note the wildly disproportionate praise this brings you – "Oh, aren't you the modern hands-on dad, doing the shopping with baby! Good for you, giving mom a rest!" Frustratingly, it still escapes some sections of the community that fathers might actually be primary caregivers.)*

**4** *Don't fall asleep on top of her after imbibing an unmemorable amount of vodka.*

Once your baby starts moving and eating solids, however, the compliments are harder to come by – and the unsolicited comments more frequent. Your mom will question the wisdom of allowing baby to play with a bottle of counter spray, and isn't at all put at ease by your indignant response, "But it's Natural Choice cleaner!"

The maternal and pediatric nurse berates you for not giving the baby enough in the way of solids, or conversely, for overfeeding her. Strangers cast judgemental sideways glances when you let her fall off the playground pony seesaw while you play Scrabble on your smartphone. And cafe proprietors give you a look that clearly suggests, "We would rather you bring your Rottweiler in here than your child."

Whether it's cultural conditioning or some evolutionary function, women seem prone to take criticism of their parenting capabilities far more personally than men. Fathers couldn't give a damn what others are thinking when they cavalierly toss their offspring in the air, or fail to clean up the encrusted cereal on baby's face. Consequently, they can get on with wasting their brainpower recalling arguably funny quotes from *Naked Gun* movies and trimming their nasal hair, rather than ruminating on what the woman at the park was implying when she asked baby where her sun hat was. So, moms, take a page out of the fellows' book and focus on the great stuff you do for your kid.

WOMEN SEEM PRONE TO TAKE CRITICISM OF THEIR PARENTING CAPABILITIES FAR MORE PERSONALLY THAN MEN

## NOT NEGLECT

Babies are beautiful, but let's get real: being in the company of a six-month-old seven days a week is hardly going to provide the mental nourishment of a David Suzuki lecture. It's not even going to provide the mental nourishment of an episode of *Two and a Half Men*. While there is great joy and satisfaction to be had in watching your baby develop, there are times when being with an infant is like sitting through a session of Congress.

Your own idea of a perfect day's activities probably doesn't involve lying on your back staring at a bug on the ceiling and repeatedly soiling yourself. But as baby gets older it becomes easier to find a happy medium between what he likes to do all day and what you like to do. Looking at dinosaur bones in the museum is fun for both of you. Watching pelicans swallow fish – also fun for both. Reading *Where is the Green Sheep?* till it haunts your every waking hour is, perhaps, not. Some days the sound of your own anodyne talking-to-the-baby voice will induce self-loathing, you'd rather stab yourself in the eye with a rusty fork than blend another round of over-boiled vegetables, and the idea of the same parents with their same preschoolers in the same playground makes you yearn for the days when the most boring thing in your life was the annual tax return.

On such days you should feel no shame in depositing baby in his playpen with a bunch of toys, a parting kiss to his forehead and a

promise that you're just in the next room with the newspaper. It's a perfectly reasonable arrangement. He doesn't care about the latest interest rate hike and you don't care how the Wiggles wake up Jeff – though you do have a few unsavory suggestions. Unfortunately, babies have a talent for making their parents feel like Pol Pot if they're left to their own devices, and will quickly learn that time in the playpen means you are temporarily AWOL. After five minutes of doodling half-heartedly with his blocks, he'll begin to vocalize in the manner of an orphaned baby wolf.

Remind yourself that leaving junior to his own devices in a sturdy wooden roofless cage is not a crime. You're not locking your little flower in an attic with his (real or imagined) sister and letting him become a starving, incestuous psychopath. And you'll be able to pull him out of his momentary abandonment blues with nothing more complicated than a juice box and yet another jolly rendition of *Where is the Green Sheep?*

(WHERE IS THE GREEN SHEEP?! YOU'RE TRYING TO TELL ME YOU REALLY DON'T KNOW WHERE THE GREEN SHEEP IS? YOU'VE HAD THE REVEAL 780 TIMES ALREADY; SURELY THERE'RE NO SURPRISES LEFT HERE, KID! I LIKE WATCHING *A CHORUS LINE* BUT I DON'T WATCH IT EVERY FUCKING NIGHT. OK, SO I DO, BUT PLEASE, PLEASE, FOR THE LOVE OF GOD, DON'T MAKE ME READ ABOUT SHEEP OF ANY SHAPE OR COLOR EVER AGAIN.)

# ON THE MOVE

Around the six-month mark you'll finally start to feel like you're gaining some understanding of the needs and wants of your baby. "Oh yes, that particular combination of screwed-up face and guttural yowl means you're hungry"; "Aha! Clenched fists and whimpers suggests to me you might be tired"; and "Staccato nose snorts and judo kicks? You're not enjoying that polyester sailor suit, are you?" This is a wonderful period: you can plonk your baby on a play mat and get on with long-neglected tasks like reorganizing the CD collection by genre or shopping online for rare vintage teacups. Baby will let you know if she needs you, but will otherwise be content to sit or lie and play with her fabric books and plastic toy cell phone.

And then she starts to crawl.

Initially there is much amusement to be had watching baby commando crawl across the carpet like Rambo edging through the Vietnamese jungle, followed by great pride as she learns to move on hands and knees. But when her first major expedition is to the open, lit fireplace or World War I weapons display cabinet, you'll realize your time of relative peace is over. From now on you'll need to constantly monitor her whereabouts and fork out for an assortment of ugly barriers, locks and baby gates. Any attractive furniture with brain-cracking sharp edges will likely go into storage, all stovetop cooking will be done on the back burners, and the laundry door will be permanently closed to prevent the consumption of cat food and fabric softener.

And just when you think you've fully baby-proofed the house and sharpened your baby-in-danger senses, your baby will start to pull herself up by grabbing onto wobbly unsecured bookcases and mobile electric heaters. While it is, of course, reassuring to know that she's developing her balance and strength, the onset of mobility sees many parents pining for the days when they could leave their baby in a room with a pair of scissors and a bottle of Campari on the floor.

Sadly, this will never again be a safe proposition, as she's now on a determined quest to master walking. The baby guides all say that at this stage you should encourage her by calling from a distance with arms outstretched. Good advice, but you will be understandably ambivalent about what your near future looks certain to entail – trying to control an individual with the same physical dexterity and capacity for reason as a bag of snakes injected with pseudoephedrine. It's not all bad news.

WHEN HER FIRST MAJOR EXPEDITION IS TO THE OPEN, LIT FIREPLACE OR WORLD WAR I WEAPONS DISPLAY CABINET, YOU'LL REALIZE YOUR TIME OF RELATIVE PEACE IS OVER

For one thing, walking is generally regarded as an important skill and it's probably best that your child learns how to do it at some point. When you need to shower, shit or shave, she can be safely installed in her crib with a whisk and a roll of toilet paper.

Until she manages to climb out of it, that is …

## PETS

Good news, lovers of difficult pets: your asthmatic Burmese or panicky whippet HAS actually taught you some valuable lessons about what to expect as a parent – primarily that the needs of your new addition take absolute precedence. Unfortunately, your pet will continue to stridently adhere to the "me first" principle irrespective of your sudden unavailability to tend to their every wish and whim.

Your pet is likely to be rather discombobulated by the arrival of baby. (To be clear, we're talking about cats and dogs here – things that live in tanks will be unfazed by their new housemate.) The transition from an open-door policy on freshly caught rodents and unlimited stroking sessions to a ban on bed sleeping and restricted lap time can induce feelings of deep abandonment in domestic animals. As much as preserving the self-esteem of an overweight poodle might not be your priority in the first few months of parenthood, it's important to reassure them that they're still loved. (It also reduces the likelihood of your pet taking up a foul new habit or anxious tic; from turning the house into a urinal to compulsively licking metallic objects, animals have many unsubtle ways of expressing their displeasure.)

It's wise to consider and take precautions against all the worst-case scenarios involving pet–baby interactions. It may be a cute sight to behold, but beware the quietly glowering cat eyeing baby as they lie side by side on the play mat. Cats will happily disembowel ducks given half a chance, so don't think they're above swiping babies on the nose. Also, try to view the bassinet, crib and stroller through the eyes of your feline: confined spaces, replete with blankets that smell like milk – what's not to love? And hey, if there's an infant in the way just lie on top of him: human heat source and immobilized enemy.

Dogs, meanwhile, may be confused as to who has priority in the pack – them or the bald squawky interloper. Make it clear to the shih tzu that baby is not a pesky younger brother they can beat up on, but another human overlord.

Of course, once you've got the pets all educated as to appropriate behavior vis-à-vis the new family member there's the arduous process of training the kid not to torture them. Riding the dog around the backyard like they're in the Indianapolis 500, dumping vats of glitter in the cat's glue-pasted ears – these are just two examples of the many and varied ways your toddler will, in time, exercise his imagination and growing physical dexterity against his furry housemate. But be comforted that you have only a few years of this behavior before child and pet will be living together in relative harmony.

Then, just as they're enjoying the extended truce after years of mutual fang-bearing and eye-gouging, Buster will come to the end of his allotted dog years and you'll be helping junior process the loss by conjuring florid tales of a fantastical canine Shangri-la.

## SHIT

Given the choice between confronting the excrement of another human being and having one's head gnawed on by a great white shark, it's fair to say a significant majority would take the option that doesn't involve getting their hands dirty. "It's different when it's your own kid's poo," people coo soothingly if you express pre-birth reservations about the handling and removal of baby shit. And while it's true you'll likely favor your kid's crap over the next-door-neighbor's any day, you're still hardly going to be high-fiving the cat before you roll up your sleeves.

Newborn diapers probably won't phase you. They smell almost sweet and are mercifully shapeless, more like an excretion of mashed-up crème brûlée than your garden-variety stinky grown-up poo. But when your baby starts ingesting mashed-up food around the six-month mark, look out! Solids = SOLIDS. Big, unwieldy, brown TURDS. If there's one area in which mindless wastage is to be acceptable, it's baby-wipe consumption. The only way to avoid getting shit on your hands is by going in with an impenetrable protective layer of wipes. One wipe just won't cut it when you're dealing with the brown stuff. Saving the forests is, of course, an urgent priority, but cut down on toilet paper, newspapers, pen pals ... anything but wipes.

If you're worried about the family budget, skimp on extraneous stuff like Moses baskets, changing tables and breastfeeding pillows. Slap a

6–12 MONTHS

cheap picture of a bunny on the nursery wall, pick up a three-pack of onesies at the supermarket, but buy great big heaving bulk boxes of wipes, for they are all that stand between you and fecal anarchy.

## SLEEP – PART TWO

You might reasonably expect that by the six- to twelve-month mark your baby will recalibrate her sleep schedule to preclude 50 squillion night wakings. She no longer occupies the moral high ground of the newly birthed, who have many valid justifications for being lousy at long stretches of sleep. Shouldn't she be exhausted from all the crawling, walking and toy-chewing she has undertaken during daylight hours? And yet many remain resolutely unmoved by their parents' increasingly ragged physical and mental state.

Desperation can set in. Drug addiction by proxy probably isn't something you anticipated as a potential hazard of parenthood, but anyone who's experienced the rush of watching a fitful, irritable baby transform into a contentedly snoring tribute to modern pharmaceuticals will have contemplated busting out the bottle of liquid-gold sleep juice, irrespective of whether there are medical grounds for it. While it sounds completely immoral, when you've not had an uninterrupted night's sleep in six months, doping your child starts to look like a less dubious practice.

There's another solution though, and one that won't make you a social pariah or compromise your baby's liver function. If you're repressing urges to sedate your baby every night and your eyes resemble cherries in milk, it might be time to get in touch with a sleep consultant.

Sleep consultants, as the name suggests, offer advice for parents whose babies wage war against slumber. They should all brandish big purple "magic happens" stickers on their front doors. To the sleep-deprived, exhausted parent close to a nervous meltdown, seeing a sleep consultant can be like a minor revelation. You are not alone. They have absolutely, honestly seen it all before.

6–12 moNtHs

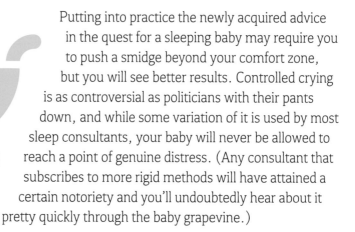

Putting into practice the newly acquired advice in the quest for a sleeping baby may require you to push a smidge beyond your comfort zone, but you will see better results. Controlled crying is as controversial as politicians with their pants down, and while some variation of it is used by most sleep consultants, your baby will never be allowed to reach a point of genuine distress. (Any consultant that subscribes to more rigid methods will have attained a certain notoriety and you'll undoubtedly hear about it pretty quickly through the baby grapevine.)

Do not expect miracles, of course, but with the right support those seemingly never-ending nights when junior just won't rest can become manageable, or even disappear altogether. So if you're the mom or dad of a stubbornly non-sleeping baby, don't be too shy or proud to get on the phone to a consultant of snooze. What have you got to lose?

# TEETH

The fantastic thing about teething is that you can attribute any bizarre or revolting behavior baby may engage in to this developmental phenomenon. Repeatedly banging his head against the crib railings = teething; chewing on the phone cord = teething; drooling like a labrador = teething; screaming all day and all night = teething.

None of these behaviors have anything to do with your child being poorly disciplined or simply odd, but are clearly the result of small sharp tombstones tunnelling their way through tender pink baby gums. And the great thing is – people believe you! Such is the fear and loathing the growth of infant teeth provokes in the entire community. However, don't overplay this card or you'll risk being The Parent Who Cried Wolf. Friends and family will extend only so much tolerance and sympathy before concluding, "No, actually your child is just a prick. I don't see any evidence of these monstrous molars you've been yammering on about for the past six months." When the little one is truly teething you'll have to draw on every morsel of support your extended network can provide, so carefully measure out those crocodile tears for when they're needed.

If you're breastfeeding, you'll likely be crying very real tears as soon as your baby puts his new chompers to no good use: "Hmmm, let's see what mommy does when I grind my front teeth against her nipple. Ohhh, tears and screams! Like mother, like son!" The little brat may even laugh at your agony. Blame his father for introducing him to the sadistic pleasures of *Reservoir Dogs*.

You'll again be reduced to toddler-like tears of frustration trying to get junior into a teeth-cleaning regimen. About 97 percent of your day's creative capacity will be spent convincing him that brushing is a FUN activity. Singing songs, pretending to be toothbrush-wielding squirrels or *Sesame Street* characters, choreographing *Dancing with the Stars*–style dance routines about the magic of sparkling canines may result in him opening his rosebud lips long enough for you to scrub away the day's food detritus. But just as likely you'll be holding down his flailing arms and legs while trying to pry open his steel-trap jaw.

Such shenanigans will make you nostalgic for the days when you only had to deal with your dog's bad breath.

# VOMIT

Humans have a unique capacity for producing foul smells, liquids and assorted bodily wastes, unrivalled by any other earth-dwelling creature. Until we're old enough to familiarize ourselves with the "vomit in bucket, poo in toilet, snot in tissue" routines, we rely on our elders to take care of all unseemly expulsions.

And when we say elders, we mean "Mostly you, mom/dad."

Daily adventures with poo and snot are relatively manageable in comparison to a bout of gastro that entails the regular, violent, upward and downward emptying of one's guts. Nothing has the power to reduce a parent to a dribbling madman more than their own spewing spawn. Even the after-effects of your own reckless participation in prolonged drinking sessions cannot prepare you for the sudden, directionless up-chucks of a toddler. Unless you craft yourself a full body condom and even if you sacrifice a bathrobe to save your mohair cardigan and black jeans,

YOU WILL, AT SOME POINT, GET COVERED IN VOMIT BY A BABY MIMICKING THE ERUPTION OF VESUVIUS you will, at some point, get covered in vomit by a baby mimicking the eruption of Vesuvius.

You can at least try to prevent your own descent into this odious hell by developing a temporary obsessive-compulsive disorder involving the incessant cleaning of hands and household surfaces. We are, vexingly, born without the wonderful self-cleaning mechanisms of a cat, but pay attention to the infuriating meticulousness with which puss washes himself after every activity. Mirror his actions – the ones that don't involve tongue-to-tush contact – and you may find yourself still standing while all and sundry around you make limpid love to the porcelain bowl, hour after miserable hour.

If, despite your best efforts, you fail to evade the gastro germs, remember this: diapers can be generous – particularly the cloth variety. An adult can squeeze their private parts into one if need be. Just sayin'.

# 12-18

## MONThS

# BACK TO WORK

Some women have very clear notions about what they'll be doing
12 months after baby's arrival – e.g., "I will definitely be donning the
Spanx and pumping breast milk in between brainstorming ways to
make kitchen splashbacks sexy and dangerous with my old team of
copywriters" or "I will unquestionably be re-creating the Funny Farm
animal party scene featured on *Sesame Street*, and spending happy
unpressured afternoons dawdling outside the zoo's meerkat enclosure."
A third group have no plan whatsoever, and bumble into some form of
paid work if it happens to be offered. For those of us who deal with the
whole parenthood/work discussion in this sort of haphazard fashion,
your authors offer three lessons learned:

### On childcare

*If, while pregnant, you were fully occupied with morning sickness,*
*comparing the circumference of the average newborn's head*
*with the width of the average female vagina, and procuring*
*designer wallpaper for the nursery, then you probably didn't pay*
*much mind to where baby would be cared for in the seemingly*
*distant future. It's hard to take these things seriously when your*

SH*T ON my HANDS

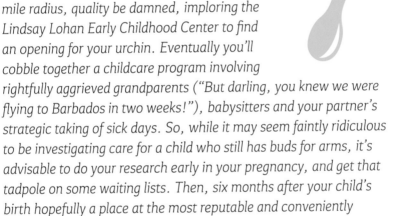

"baby bump" still looks like the result of too much pasta and Budweiser rather than fetal invasion. Consequently, three days before your unexpectedly offered work contract commences, you'll find yourself frantically ringing every day-care center within a 50-mile radius, quality be damned, imploring the Lindsay Lohan Early Childhood Center to find an opening for your urchin. Eventually you'll cobble together a childcare program involving rightfully aggrieved grandparents ("But darling, you knew we were flying to Barbados in two weeks!"), babysitters and your partner's strategic taking of sick days. So, while it may seem faintly ridiculous to be investigating care for a child who still has buds for arms, it's advisable to do your research early in your pregnancy, and get that tadpole on some waiting lists. Then, six months after your child's birth hopefully a place at the most reputable and conveniently located childcare provider will be available for you to accept or graciously reject.

## On mental preparation

The stay-at-homers know from the outset of their child's gestation that they will not be facing a harried daily commute to and from *work via the day-care, but the back-to-worker can be shell-shocked by their sudden reality – speeding tickets, missed buses, unsympathetic bosses and, upon discovering the slow cooker has apparently had a midday power outtage, challenging the baby to a who-can-have-the-loudest-tantrum-on-the-kitchen-floor duel. So, while contemplating the girth of your nipples during night feeds, try to imagine what it might be like to rejoin the workforce. Even if you don't end up back at work in the short term, you've a better chance at not coming undone by the new kind of psychic upset that a day in the workplace with no sleep and a pee stain on your skirt can induce.*

### On minding your own business

*At all costs, avoid participating in the "Mommy Wars." This is a phenomenon whereby seemingly rational women flail each other in online forums, newspaper columns and books about when and if mothers of young kiddies should return to work. Ignore all this unseemly carping and get on with doing what's right for you. And once you've made your decision, strenuously avoid becoming a loopy crusader for whichever side of the fence you've settled on for the time being. There are clearly legitimate reasons for women to get back into the workplace (terrifying mortgage/rent; resuming successful career), just as there are good reasons for many not to (partner has more money than God; prefer the company of offspring to colleagues; don't feel ready to put baby in childcare). Just remember to enjoy the benefits that come with either decision.*

## SLEEP – PART THREE

There's a glorious period after your baby starts sleeping through the night when bedtime is a relatively simple affair. A bit of warm milk, a couple of cozy bedtime tales, a big hug, and voilà, baby falls asleep. You'll have the pleasure of eavesdropping on your child as he puts himself to sleep with some sublimely sweet and ridiculous self-soothing rituals: fake snoring; singing loud tuneless lullabies with creative lyrical maulings; recapping the day's activities with his own peculiar slant on events.

By 7:30 p.m. you'll be happily ensconced in the adult pursuit of your choice, secure in the knowledge that nothing short of a yodelling contest will prompt your baby to wake.

And then one evening the malevolent fairy of prolonged sleep rituals will visit him, sprinkle glittery pixie dust all over his pillows and whisper into his ear, "You know, you really must learn how to fuck with your parents a bit more at bedtime." Enthusiastically embracing the idea, your young one will begin to craft his evening routine into one of eye-wateringly drawn out monotonous frustration: requests for umpteen blanket rearrangements, glasses of water, one more book, another goodnight kiss for the cat, a belly rub.

In time you'll learn how to short-circuit all the procrastination devices your child has up his sleeve. Present the cat for a one-time only opportunity to say goodnight. Reassure your child that even if there was such a thing as monsters, they'd find it impossible to access his room due to the child safety gate at the top of the stairs. It takes craft and cunning, but slowly the demands will recede as your child again grudgingly accepts that you've had an encounter with your own supernatural sprite, albeit one who's ditched the Tinkerbell wings for prison-warden britches.

# CHILDCARE

If you're a stay-at-home parent, particularly a single one, don't feel you're taking the soft option if you put your child in day care a couple of days a week. You may imagine people turning up their noses in disdain and humiliating you in hairdressing salons – "Aahh, so THIS is what you do all day! Tough life for some, eh?" There's a simple and highly effective retort to any mockery of this sort: "You work five days a week and enjoy a two-day weekend. I have two eight-hour blocks a week in which to do everything that is difficult with a toddler in tow, which is everything. Also, your haircut makes you look like an electrocuted sheepdog."

Aside from your entirely justifiable need for an occasional break from your child, day-care centers can provide two important services: stimulation and socialization.

There are people who believe they can provide all the stimulation their child requires in their own home, but not everyone has a backyard replete with chickens, vegetable garden, sandpit, swings, cubby and tricycles. And if you live in a small rental apartment with wall-to-wall carpet and a kitchen the size of a neoconservative's prefrontal cortex, dazzlingly messy craft and baking projects are off-limits. Other people may scorn your anxiety about your abilities to keep

## YOUR OFFSPRING CAN ACQUIRE THE NICETIES OF SOCIAL INTERACTION: SHARING, PATIENCE, LISTENING AND THE BEST PLACE TO DISCREETLY SMEAR ONE'S NASAL EMISSIONS

your child entertained: "Let her get bored," they opine. This is sound advice when dealing with a mopey teen, who when bored might do something constructive like fashion a bucket bong out of laundry supplies. But toddlers? They will entertain themselves beautifully with their tea set for half an hour, then they will flush a tennis ball down the toilet and pee in the heating vents. Childcare centers score big points for being hives of creative, untidy activities. And someone other than you always cleans up afterwards – that's why they're expensive.

Their other great benefit is that they are, unsurprisingly, full of other children, thus facilitating infinite opportunities for socialization. With extended families tending to live farther and farther apart, and profligate breeding no longer the norm, get-togethers with hordes of similarly aged children may be a rare occurrence. Playgroups and parents' groups are fantastic, but only provide a few hours' interaction each week at best. Making the acquaintance of neighbors with kids is a great idea, too, but if your neighbors are perpetually drugged Deadheads and gently demented retirees, you're a bit stuck. Childcare centers, teeming as they may be with plastic furniture, laminated surfaces and gastrointestinal viruses, are a space in which your offspring can acquire the niceties of social interaction: sharing, patience, listening and the best place to discreetly smear one's nasal emissions.

## CONSTIPATION

Sunday newspapers are quite partial to the old "What I did last night" or "My Perfect Sunday" columns, in which a minor TV star or musician shares details of their weekend of blissed-out sleep-ins and lazy brunches at semi-rural restaurants followed by pleasantly wine-soaked afternoon gigs. Never do these individuals include on their lists of fun weekend pursuits: "spent entire weekend a slave to the fluctuating moods of a habitually constipated toddler."

Constipated babies and toddlers express their backed-up distress by shedding tears, flailing arms, hurling toy blocks and kicking kindly grandmother-types who make the mistake of sharing a footpath with them. Hell hath no fury like that of an 18-month-old with the equivalent of a house brick stuck in his lower intestine. He knows this wretched waste is going to have to come out some time soon, that it's bigger than his head, and accordingly this gives him license to bitch in much the same way premenstrual tension gives his mother an excuse for being a bloated wailing witch.

But oh the satisfaction when at long last that series of brown grenades gets tossed from its bunker and your sobbing, traumatized little one clutches at you with blessed relief, finally able to enjoy an unbroken night's sleep in comfort. This is about as perfect a Sunday as you can hope for with a young family.

## MENSTRUATION

One day you'll be sitting on the toilet, quietly attending to your excretory needs, when, ye gads, you'll realize there's a bloodstain on the crotch of your underwear. After nine months of pregnancy and up to a year of motherhood, all blessedly period-free, this may come as quite a shock. You might even wonder if this is more post-birth bleeding – though it's been practically a year since baby's arrival. So unfamiliar are you with the menstrual experience that you might find yourself having painfully vivid flashbacks to that day in sixth grade when you realized you were a woman, and that you were demonstrating the fact all over the back of your favorite school dress.

Snapping out of your childhood flashback you finally come to grips with the fact that the crimson wave has crashed again and you need a tampon. There must be one here SOMEWHERE. Bathroom drawers, old handbags, filing cabinets and those decorative boxes filled with rubber bands and antifungal cream for the cat yield nothing. With a wad of scratchy toilet paper stuffed into your de-elasticized underpants, off you trot to the drugstore. Expect to be struck dumb by the expanded array of ridiculously colored and patterned tampons. Also expect to pay the equivalent of a tank of gas for a period's worth of protection.

Safely home and hovering over the toilet, it may take you a good few minutes to figure out how to remove the damned tampon's plastic covering – "Aha, so they've changed to a twist-and-pull method!" – but finally your underwear, skirt and armchairs are safe from the menstrual flow. But wait, do you have any ibuprofen? Bah-bam. Best be dusting off that old copy of *Seventeen* and reacquainting yourself with the finer points of what happens when a girl becomes a woman.

# SINGLE MOTHERHOOD

It's unlikely you'll encounter many people proffering chirpy affirmations about the benefits of single motherhood: "Single motherhood? No sweat! As easy as eating ice cream on a sunny day." Parenting guidebooks, when they deign to toss out a few paragraphs on the subject, give the impression that while perhaps not quite on a par with locking your child in a cellar and blasting polka music through a loudspeaker, children of single moms can still look forward to a future of maladjusted misery.

Regardless of how confident you are in your own abilities as a parent this can be demoralizing. Contrary to popular wisdom you might actually feel pretty okay about being a single mom. Not every Ms. is sobbing into her soup after she puts the baby to bed, yearning for Y-fronts in her lingerie drawer and a shared bank account.

In fact, you may have chosen from the outset to undertake parenting alone. Maybe you accidentally stored the sperm of a one-night stand in your uterus and decided "to hell with restrictive social norms. I'm having this baby. I hope it inherits what's-his-name's nice cheekbones." Or perhaps you used donor sperm after realizing you wanted a baby and weren't going to waste time waiting for a willing and suitable man to come along.

You could also be a single mom because your relationship broke up. It's this scenario that tends to cause the most guilt, anxiety and hand-wringing. But the self-blame should be disposed of like the radioactive waste it is. Your child is much better off with two homes rather than with one in which his parents are

## SINGLE MOTHERHOOD? NO SWEAT! AS EASY AS EATING ICE-CREAM ON A SUNNY DAY

at best nonplussed with each other and at worst waging World War III. Kids are smart, despite their well-documented tendencies to crap themselves and engage happily with the *Teletubbies*. They know when you're miserable. As long as they're treated with love and respect they'll get through a break-up with few if any permanent scars. They're much more likely to suffer long-term damage by witnessing the unique kind of misery that haunts the unhappily shacked up.

Once you've negotiated a shared- or sole-custody arrangement, the benefits will come to light. There's the opportunity to create an even more intimate bond with your child, and the pride that comes from making it through an undeniably rattling experience. There's the relief at being able to do things (mostly) on your own terms. And should shared parenting be the arrangement, the chance for extended breaks from the demands of full-time parenting.

Of course, it can feel like your arm's been cut off when you first relinquish your child to their other parent. But note the awe and envy

12–18 MONTHS

of partnered parents when you regale them with tales of drinking like a fish and dancing wildly on a Saturday night. Unlike you, they can't spend entire Sunday mornings lolling in bed recovering from a hangover, and so must resign themselves to weekly squabbles about whether it's burrito or pizza night. And think about the women catatonic from round-the-clock parenting, year-in, year-out, granted only a couple of hours off on Sundays when their workaholic partner takes the baby to the park.

Being a single parent isn't easy. But neither is being a married one.

## SWIMMING LESSONS

After you become a parent the nightly news may as well be called "terrible things that could happen to your child." Backyard pool drownings are an all-too-common occurrence and, heeding the cautionary tales, it's likely you'll be signing your offspring up for swimming lessons before you've cleaned the mucous plug stain off the car seat. But the local swimming pool will tell you to go away for another six months at least and, inevitably overwhelmed by all the other stuff crowding your first year of parenthood, baby will likely be able to say "swim", "water wings" and "novelty inflatable crocodile" before she's actually had any direct contact with chlorine.

When you do finally begin swimming lessons, two things will become immediately apparent:

**1** *Babies love water. Of course they do. They're not the ones crossing their legs underwater when they realize their pubic hair needs a swimsuit of its own, or that an unwieldy penis is creeping out of its appropriate position in unsupported trunks.*

**2** *Adults gain almost nothing from the experience, save the initial rush of seeing their baby in teeny tiny swimsuits. There is something uniquely bothersome about the time and effort required to travel to the pool, get the both of you undressed and water-ready, and then repeat the whole process in reverse at the other end.*

But give up you cannot. The "CHILD DROWNS IN RIVER: PARENTS SIMPLY COULDN'T BE BOTHERED WITH SWIMMING LESSONS" headlines will compel you to keep dragging out those swimsuits week after week. A healthy way to improve your outlook is to pretend you're someone else. At the next lesson, focus on that mom or dad of a sporty, sunny disposition who actually seems to be enjoying themselves. Invite them for a cup of rat-shit coffee at the pool cafe, and pry out the secret of their happy attitude. You'll learn that as a youngster, swimming was their life; they were a state and national 100-yard butterfly titleholder. During their university years they gave up the Olympic dream for a life in spa promotions, but never lost their love of the lap lane. Where others wrinkle their nose at the chlorine fog that greets them at the heated indoor pool, it sets their adrenaline pumping. And should their little boy pursue competitive swimming, they could think of nothing better than spending glorious spring weekends inside a dank swimming complex.

This is the person whose identity you need to adopt when swim day rolls around each week. As you pull out the sodden beach towels from the bottom of the laundry basket, picture yourself thrilled by baby's ability to hold a foam stick in water, hold a cup in water and wear a diaper in water. Imagine yourself cheerfully thanking the teacher at the end of the class rather than moaning about the fluctuating pool temperature and what chlorine does to your hair dye job.

And next time you see a news item concerning water and children that sends chills down your spine, you'll be able to soothe yourself with the knowledge that your child is very confident singing "Baa Baa Black Sheep" in water.

# TALKING

"Dada." "Mama." "Hat." "Cat." "Puppy." "Blanket." "Fuckit." Both the beauty and the horror of small children is that they really are the sponges neuroscientists tell us they are. Unfortunately your noble efforts to teach your little boy the alphabet in French will be remarked upon far less than your inability to protect his young ears from your own profanity-laced speech. The pride you feel when baby forms his first proper word will be matched by the shame you feel when, as a confidently conversant toddler, he drops the ill-judged F-bomb into a stranger's ear.

Shiny young cherubs spouting swear words have the power to shock their elders in much the same way as a nun wearing hot pants. It's by turns funny, unsettling and inappropriate. And nobody will buy your story that he learned the offending word from a foul-mothed lunatic at the bus stop.

This seemingly innate ability to identify and repeat bad words is predominantly a phase of early toddlerhood, so don't get too hung-up on cleaning up your own mouth. Swear words act in a similar way

**"DADA."**
**"MAMA."**
**"HAT." "CAT."**
**"PUPPY."**
**"BLANKET."**
**"FUCKIT."**

12–18 months

# 'I DON'T PEE IN THE BATH BECAUSE I'M A VEGETARIAN'

to germs: repeated exposure builds up children's immunity to them, and, by the age of two, parroting your road-rage rants will be abandoned in favor of giddy chatter about pirates in tutus. This is when conversations become a truly loopy two-way street. Your child's unbridled fantasy world, which they've probably occupied from Day One, is now something they can effectively communicate to you. Every parent has their own treasure trove of beautifully charming toddler utterances. While few people will think your child's declaration that "I don't pee in the bath because I'm a vegetarian" is the pinnacle of genius wordplay, to you it's evidence of a uniquely whimsical and gifted personality.

Relish every brilliant proclamation, for these are the glory years when your child's speech is a source of delight. Hold these memories close to your heart in their teen years, when communication is restricted to a series of muffled grunts, and words they learned when you were trying to parallel park the Volvo all those years ago.

# TELEVISION AND iGADGETS

*"Oh, I just don't understand how anyone could let their kids watch two hours of TV a day! I mean, really, what kind of a parent does that?"*

What kind of a parent? The one who recognizes that when their kid rises at 5:30 a.m. and goes to bed at 8 p.m., two hours of TV is a mere fraction of their daily activities. While there are some marvelous beings out there who will happily spend dusk till dawn cutting and pasting, whizzing down slides at the playground, baking haphazardly charming gingerbread men and ploughing through the collected works of Dr. Seuss, for most of us the TV provides one of the only true opportunities to unfurl the child curled around our leg and get on with a few things.

Many a child would never have experienced the joys of a hot meal without the TV to distract them from their usual routine of excruciatingly pitched whining and ankle biting. Their clothes would never have been treated to the lemon-scented wonders of a heavy cycle in the washing machine, and the carpet in their home would resemble that of an abandoned disco.

BUT WHAT ABOUT iGADGETS? ... DON'T ASK US. DON'T ASK ANYONE

12–18 MONTHS

## WITH ANY LUCK, THE NEXT GENERATION'S LOVE AFFAIR WITH GADGETRY WILL BE SOMEWHAT LESS FERVENT THAN OURS

As long as your kid spends part of each day running around, reading and inventing complex personalities for clothespins, why should you feel guilty about letting them watch *Sesame Street*? Television, despite the many crimes against intelligence and good taste committed in its name, is not inherently evil. Keep them well away from advertisements for obesity-inducing foods and IQ-sapping toys, and you'll find TV can actually benefit rather than stymie their florid young imaginations. There are new words, ideas and concepts to be gleaned. Go on, switch on that TV. Remember, if it's produced by a public broadcaster, it's EDUCATIONAL. As for you, go ahead and indulge in a bit of *Rock of Love with Bret Michaels*. You've already completed your education, after all.

But what about iGadgets? What age/how much time/what's suitable? Don't ask us. Don't ask ANYONE. They'll lie about their own children's usage, just as they fudge the truth when the doctor asks how many units of alcohol they consume per week. Be particularly wary of the opinion of older generations. Condemn as they may the infiltration of technology into their grandkids' lives, in the '50s and '60s they gawped with equally sweet wonder at *Leave it to Beaver* and *Mister Ed*.

With any luck, the next generation's love affair with gadgetry will be somewhat less fervent than ours: "My mom told me that in her day, people couldn't take a crap without simultaneously scrolling through their Twitter feed! I mean, their bowels actually just SEIZED UP!"

# 18-24

## months

# AFFECTION

Very few relationships go the distance when one party is blazingly affectionate and the other has all the responsive capabilities of a cactus. Your little one doubtless appreciates and benefits from your impassioned declarations of love and nighttime butterfly kisses, but he's likely to take his own sweet time in learning the value of reciprocal gestures. Until he decides to chime in with an "I love you," you may feel you've regressed to your awkward teenage years when the target of your passion either humorously tolerated or flat-out rejected your lovelorn entreaties.

In fact, babies can be far crueller in their refusals of slobbering parental love. They swipe at your puckered lips, demand to be put down when you hold them on your lap and squirm as if they were being invited to embrace Satan himself when you attempt to lock them in a cuddle. And if you're feeling forlorn about the current political climate or Clinique discontinuing its matte lipstick in terra-cotta (WHY?), your baby can reliably be counted on to offer you zilch in the way of comfort.

Then, seemingly out of the blue, your kid will decide to tap into his inner romantic hero. One "I love you" a day will not suffice. You will be told you are loved when you present him with a burnt piece of toast. You will be smothered with kisses at every turn. He will have finally cottoned on to the idea that affection is best enjoyed mutually. With some alarm you'll find yourself prone on the couch while your child clambers aboard to reenact Hollywood-style clinches, complete with happy sighs and moans. Where previously you were pathetically grateful for some prolonged eye contact, you now contemplate explaining the concept of "personal space." But mostly his starry-eyed declarations will thrill you. They're ample reward for all those months you spent giving him subtle prompts to worship you like: "Say you love Mommy. You love Mommy, don't you? SAY I LOVE MOMMY!"

# DISCIPLINE

Independence is a wonderful thing. The day your kid learns to open the cereal box and switch the TV on by herself is truly a miracle on a par with birth itself. Independence, alas, also brings with it a whole new slew of problems that'll have you ripping out your pubic hair in the shower.

Babies aren't so bad: they respond to every word you say like excited puppy dogs, and are chiefly concerned with eating toilet paper

## BABIES ... RESPOND TO EVERY WORD YOU SAY LIKE EXCITED PUPPY DOGS, AND ARE CHIEFLY CONCERNED WITH EATING TOILET PAPER AND DUST

and dust, rather than asserting their own egos. But by the time they're approaching their second year out of the womb, they're starting to have a better idea of your foibles and failings. As with any long-term relationship there comes a point when those rose-colored glasses come off and your child thinks, "What have you done for ME lately?"

Now rest assured that once the bright shiny glow of her babyhood love dims a little, she won't act up the way your old flame did when they became less than enthralled by you – seeking BJs from 20-year-olds. She'll just decide to close her ears to every gentle, firm request for compliance. She'll become immune to bribery, laugh in the face of threats, pay no heed to your own reactive tantrums, and be smug and contrary when you plead.

It's hard not to give them a whack on the bottom sometimes, but it's not a route most of us go down, and for good reasons – though older family members might grumble that they got the odd slap and they're fine. That crazy Uncle who used to get a belting when he wet the bed and now thinks his penis is something to stir his tea with provides compelling evidence to the contrary. Hitting kids is bullshit, plain and simple.

The best way to learn about effective discipline is to watch a qualified child-care teacher work her magic in the eye of a toddler shit storm. It's amazing what can be achieved by getting down on the child's level, establishing eye contact, and speaking in a calm, low, firm voice. Or go to the vet and observe them wrangling a couple of overly excited schnoodles. The same principle applies: remain composed and remove the beasts from the source of angst.

If, however, your child is on a bad behavior bender and no amount of calm remonstrations are working, turn to social networking. Post a pithy but appropriately desperate status update declaring you are at breaking point and be comforted by the stories that come back to you: "My sister is going through the same thing"; "The neighbors called the police when I was washing my daughter's hair last night"; "I swallowed a fly on my lunch break today."

And while waiting for those sanity-saving wall posts, close your eyes, breathe deeply and try to infiltrate your child's mind-set: "Yes, I too would be frustrated if my language skills were rudimentary and people presented me with raisins when I was clearly requesting bananas. Of course I would be reticent to wear long sleeves in winter when it's all of 35°F outside and the apartment feels like a storage unit for frozen chickens. And no, I definitely wouldn't want to brush my teeth when I could revel in the aftertaste of my dinner all night long. It makes perfect sense. No, it doesn't. It makes as much sense as soft lighting in an operating room. There is something wrong with my child. It must be because I ate feta cheese during my pregnancy. Perhaps after I imbibe this bottle of cheap wine I'll be in the right frame of mind to understand it."

# DISABILITY

Unless you've previously had a predilection for bondage and discipline, pregnancy and birth will be the first experience you have of relinquishing control and accepting that your future is now in the hands of another human being. The most daunting aspect of reproduction is the question "what if?" And for a small number of people, the "what if" becomes "what now?"

Nobody much likes to discuss unexpected diagnoses at birth, neurological disorders, nor the expectation of physical perfection – or something close to it – that we hold for our progeny. That's not a criticism. You're not a monster if you hope your child won't have a disability. And you're not a monster if, when your child does turn out to have a disability, you don't immediately react with acceptance and resolve. It's very likely you'll spend periods loathing your friends with physically and neurologically sound and healthy kids – particularly when they have the audacity to *complain* about them to you. You'll also probably be prone to bouts of deep self-pity.

While some people might tell you to get over yourself, we say let it all hang the fuck out emotionally for as long as you need. Because yes, you have been dealt a shitty card and it's completely natural to wonder why. You have lost the future you expected, and your daily life is probably damned difficult in many ways. But, as a particularly wonderful nurse told one of us when such a diagnosis was delivered, "You've still *got* your child, and you *do* have the strength to advocate for her." Tough, but true.

Having a child with a disability is a real life changer, but not all for the worst. Every day you'll be startled by the achievements they make beyond what you imagined their capacities to be. The level of compassion, intelligence and assistance provided by underpaid (mostly female) disability support providers and early intervention workers will also alter your worldview for the better, as will the bonds you'll form with other parents in your situation. Parents of children with disabilities tend to have a uniquely macabre and deeply enjoyable sense of humor, plus that much-longed-for "perspective" we all strive for but seldom achieve.

# FOOD BATTLES

When the time comes to raise that first spoonful of solids to your baby's milk-mustached mouth, you'll probably have some idea of the sorts of things you would and would not like them to eat. Sweets and hot dogs = bad. Whole-wheat pasta and broccoli = good. Your kid will probably comply for a while and devour plates brimming with whole grains and greens: "Aren't you a good baby", you'll coo proudly, "you'll never be a sugar-crazed ratbag. I, your parent, will always prepare you nutritious foods that you will continue to happily ingest for the rest of your days. You'll probably initiate world peace, too."

Frustratingly, this dreamy setup will probably go to hell after his first year. A percentage of kids will continue to eat everything on the bottom two rungs of the food pyramid, but a greater proportion will be steadfast in their refusal to eat anything but Cheerios, cheese, white bread, crackers, white chocolate, white bread, cheese, crackers, Cheerios, cheese, crackers, cookies, cheese, crackers and white bread. Once children realize that crap food is fun, trying to lead them back down the leafy-greens path is a fearsome undertaking. Dinnertime can rapidly become the most hateful part of your day. Holes kicked in the pantry door and silent directives to "eat a bowl of FUCK, kiddo!" are an entirely rational response when you've wasted half your weekly earnings on new and exciting foods to tempt your child's white supremacist taste buds.

When you've lived through 30-odd years of ups and downs it's difficult to understand how the sight of a broccoli stem could reduce anyone to tears, but toddlers have yet to learn that life contains far more vexing problems than

**ONCE CHILDREN REALIZE THAT CRAP FOOD IS FUN, TRYING TO LEAD THEM BACK DOWN THE LEAFY-GREENS PATH IS A FEARSOME UNDERTAKING**

unwanted vegetables. He will learn, eventually, that there are foods worth eating beyond butter pats and toothpaste. Getting children to subscribe to the old "don't judge a book by its cover" mantra is the hardest part – once they've actually tasted what you're offering, they're often less likely to reject it.

So, pretend he's a rat and scatter bits of healthy grub about the lounge room; eventually he'll start to nibble. Trying to force your kid to eat well 24/7 is not worth the headaches, the frown lines and mutual tantrums. Avoid food battles because he actually can survive and even thrive for a time on crackers, and banish any bad feelings about his diet by digging up the yard and using all the money you've saved on fresh produce to install a guitar-shaped swimming pool.

# NUMBER TWO

You'll find getting pregnant again a little like being offered the opportunity to go on *Who Wants to Be a Millionaire* a second time. "Yes!" you think triumphantly, "Bring it on! I know so much more now! THIS TIME I WON'T FUCK IT UP!"

Yet many expectant second timers worry that they will not be able to replicate the same euphoric love they experienced with their first child. Should you admit to any ambivalence about your pregnancy, be prepared for people to say things like "your heart has room for more than one child." As corny as it sounds, they're actually correct. You might struggle initially to forge the same bond with your second baby (especially if they were a 12-pound vaginally delivered number), but one day you actually will wake up and think "I can't wait to see that squished fatty face." The love you feel for number two may not precisely replicate what you feel for your first, but that doesn't make it a lesser one.

If you feel completely overwhelmed by the arrival of baby redux – and it is very, very normal to feel this way – remember this: you are taking part in a marathon, and all marathons end. Even Sting and Trudie Styler had to put their underpants back on, eventually, and attend to matters other than prolonged mutual orgasm. Your days of barbaric servitude will eventually evolve into an altogether more organized and joyous chaos.

## PLAYGROUNDS

If you thought the closest you'd ever come to reliving your high school years was engaging in a happy few hours of Facebook stalking (there's nothing so gratifying as discovering that your acid-tongued high school tormentor is now boring the world to tears with relentless updates regarding her son's toilet training – "Tyson did number 2s on the potty today! So proud lol!"), then motherhood may take you by surprise. Once you start doing the rounds of the local playgrounds you'll find a scene that seems every bit as hierarchical as a private girls' school. Only now the stakes are higher. It's not "Did you bring your dad's valium to school?" but "Did you bid on that architecturally remodelled pig pen? It went for a song – only 1.5 mil!"

Women at the playground cluster in groups just as obviously demarcated as in high school: skinny rich bitches, good-natured nerds with limp hair, and all the rest, generally identified by their pleasantly bemused facial expressions that signal their uncertainty about how to penetrate this new social strata.

Happily at some point you'll realize that your acceptance into these cliques matters much less to you than it did back in the days of saddle shoes and poodle skirts. Even more happily, you'll find things have relaxed somewhat since high school, and some of those seemingly snarly looking types are actually quite nice, and that they too haven't slept in two years. Indeed, you may even pick up some new neighborhood friends. This is, in fact, crucial, for it is extremely useful to have a network of local parents.

But most importantly of all, the playground is there so that your kid will expend enough energy to collapse in a heap at 7 p.m. and sleep for 12 hours straight. Food, sex, running water, fitting in with the crowd – these all come distant seconds to an unbroken night's sleep.

# SINGLE FATHERHOOD

Scant attention is paid to you, you poor fellows. The only time we hear of single dads in the media is when some misguided soul draws attention to their divorced fathers' support group (generally thinly veiled exercises in rampant misogyny) by stalking their ex online or holding a comically dour protest outside their ex's house, or when they threaten to throw themselves off an elevated location. Of course, the anguish of a father unwillingly separated from his children is not to be sneezed at. But with the cooperation of your ex there's no reason to assume that shared parenting can't be achieved.

Very small children are a bit hairy, figuratively speaking. Shuttling baby back and forth between homes may not be a terrific idea – it's very hard to get any fail-safe guidance on shared custody arrangements for babies – but setting aside regular blocks of time each week to spend with them certainly is. The thousands of tomes devoted to separated parents don't seem to pay much mind to the matter of infants caught in the middle of a split; instead their emphasis tends to be on kids old enough to articulate feelings such as "you suck" and "I want to live with dad because he doesn't make me have flaxseed oil on my oatmeal."

While keeping your baby for stretches of days at a time may not be feasible when they're very small, rest assured that as they mature and enter the preschool years this becomes a much more realistic prospect. The advantages of these periods of solo parenting cannot be underestimated. Your bond with your child naturally becomes more intense when you're their exclusive caregiver for days on end, and your competence in pigtail-maintenance, bottom-wiping and bedtime settling will skyrocket. The sniping and snitching about minor differences of opinion regarding the day-to-day minutiae of child rearing ("I wouldn't let him jump on that bed in those shoes … Why are his clothes all muddy? … Don't feed him chocolate before dinner … *Clockwork Orange* is not appropriate viewing for a two-year-old …" etc., etc.) are a blessed thing of the past, too – especially if the ex resides in a comfortably distant suburb.

It's an unfortunate reality that while men tend not to put "has children from a previous relationship" at the top of their list of Ideal Partner requirements, women seem to be less fazed by, and even rather attracted to, men who have a child. It's irrefutable proof that they're hooked up correctly in the testicle department and may be tempted to tread that road again.

# TANTRUMS

A light magnolia scent with a top note of sandalwood fills the air. Rack upon rack of remarkably crafted designer dresses await your gleeful inspection. Soft French pop-music sounds hum sweet and low from the speakers. Thoughtfully flattering lighting creates the illusion you're 17 again. A toddler lies spread-eagled on the marble floors, eyes clenched shut, fists slugging the air, screaming "but I want a BARBIE BAND-AID NOW!!!!!!"

Nothing is likelier to shake off any pesky middle-class niceties your Catholic school education has burdened you with than dealing with your drooling freak of a child in a department store or supermarket. Your logical, educated brain tells you to kneel gently before the urchin and inform her softly but firmly that "this is a very unseemly outburst; kindly cease your wailing at once."

Unfortunately, your logical frontal lobe isn't usually the one that takes charge in these mortifyingly public displays of bad behavior. Indeed, your feelings are more likely to resemble Uncle Monty's in *Withnail and I*, when he declares of his cat, "Once again that oaf has destroyed my day. It will die, it will DIE!" Except that Uncle Monty is an iconic cinematic creation, while you are a red-faced turnip in a highly public

space screaming "I've had fucking enough, you disgusting pill of a child!"

It happens to everyone. Really, it does. Parents of babies don't generally understand this. They observe toddlers losing their shit in the soft-drink aisle, cradle their downy-haired bundle to their chest and think quietly to themselves: "My kid will never do anything as awful as that. She's so placid and sweet." Rest assured, good parenting does not immunize a child against tantrums.

The most tried-and-true way to quell the high-pitched rantings of a catatonic two-year-old is to make a joke of it. Attempting to reason with them is like trying to teach a cat origami. If you make them laugh, you'll stop the reactor from melting. Distraction, distraction, distraction … all the way to the door. In all likelihood getting them to giggle will entail making a fool of yourself – licking your nose with your tongue, pretending your smartphone's in your undies – but better to look like a fool than have a child who makes fertile young things run for the nearest sterilization clinic.

# TOILET TRAINING

Your preparation for toilet training should commence before you conceive. If you're in the midst of upgrading your furniture or floor coverings, and you hear the siren call of your underworked womb imploring you to breed, save yourself a future interior breakdown by staying away from fabric couches, pale-colored carpet and anything that can't be cleaned with steel wool. Go for vinyl, bare floorboards and cheap, dark, densely patterned rugs. Sure, your digs may look more like a desert whorehouse than a chic spa resort, but at least you'll be prepared when the excretions start to fly.

And fly they will. His liberation from diapers, fascination with squishy substances and propensity to throw stuff will combine to result in some dire situations. Never enquire as to what object the young master is examining in his hand if it is on the butterscotch-to-brown end of the color spectrum. If it looks like it might be poo, it is. Don't think he isn't contemplating tossing it your way so you might admire its textural and olfactory qualities, too.

Keep in mind also the need to protect the integrity of the child's car seat and stroller for the (hopefully brief) period it takes him to realize that the toilet is not teeming with flesh-eating monsters and is actually a far more civilized way of approaching waste management than wearing bulky and bothersome poo catchers. A handy tool for this purpose is the plastic mat from the expensive designer portable diaper-changing kit you bought as an excited parent-to-be and used twice.

Be super-wary of taking a diaper-less toddler on public transport during the toilet-training stage. Saddam Hussein was the target of less loathing than you will be if the kid poos his pants on a rush-hour train.

# TOYS

Interior design magazines can reliably be counted on to contain photographs of beautifully restored Modernist homes bursting at the seams with the finest mid-century Danish furniture and objets d'art. Do you see a hot-pink plastic bin full of Fisher-Price's finest taking pride of place next to the Børge Mogensen high-backed easy chair? No, you don't.

Much as you may aspire to reside in such digs, your child would prefer to live in a jumping castle. She will gradually accumulate certain possessions that shatter all your stylish aspirations. For the objects that stimulate toddlers – toys – generally hold all the aesthetic appeal of a portable toilet. Toys are like cockroaches – slowly but surely they'll colonize your home. You'll wake up with them on your face. You'll find them in the dishwasher. They'll surprise you under pillows. While you could conceive of a house strewn with artfully placed knitted kittens, liberty-print teddy bears and vintage dolls' baby buggies, your child's favorite toys will be things that make you want to cut your ears off and poke your eyes out.

Does it produce noises so shatteringly high-pitched only dogs and Mariah Carey can hear them? "Gimme, gimme, gimme, please, mom." Did an exploited Third World factory worker probably make it? "I'll have one in red and one in purple, dad." Does it reinforce the most putrid of gender stereotypes? "Please, mom? Pleeeeaaaaase can I have it, please?"

When you start living with a partner, compromises regarding taste become a reality: you can display your vintage dentistry gear in the dining room if I can put my "Meat is Murder" art project in the bathroom. Now you have to work out toy compromises with your

**FOR THE OBJECTS THAT STIMULATE TODDLERS – TOYS – GENERALLY HOLD ALL THE AESTHETIC APPEAL OF A PORTABLE TOILET**

18–24 MONtHS

113

child: you can have the singing plastic play table if you agree to actively engage with the wooden sushi set I bought you. Have the Dora kitchen, but know that when we have guests I'm bringing out the pale blue French Le Toy Van one. Noble ideas of maintaining a house free of plastic toys will be partially if not fully abandoned when you realize that a wooden car will buy you ten minutes of peace while a plastic ride-on monster truck will buy you an hour.

Everything, eventually, is measured in minutes of peace.

## TRAVEL

It's said that playing classical music to your unborn enhances their future capacity for learning and empathy. But where is the research that tells expectant parents what they can do to improve their child's ability to remain placid during four-hour car trips and 16-hour stints on airplanes? Who wouldn't trade a few IQ points for a happy traveller?

Travelling with children is one of the primary reasons the childless-by-choice are childless by choice. Children tend to react to air travel as if they were being placed in a giant flying coffin, with all the attendant squirming and tears you would expect of one being buried alive. By the end of an international flight, you will probably need a coffin of your own.

Advice? Just. Don't. Do. It. Restrict your air time until the baby is old enough to embrace the opportunity to watch unlimited in-flight movies.

**KIDS UNDER TWO MAY TRAVEL FREE, BUT THERE IS A VERY HIGH PRICE TO PAY INDEED**

Kids under two may travel free, but there is a very high price to pay indeed. If you must travel with l'enfant, try to do it with an airline desperate enough for your patronage that they've transformed their fleet into winged day-care centers (some actually now employ nannies to wrangle little kids).

Cars are far harder to avoid. Some babies love the car, and for others still, it's an essential requirement for sleep. Equally, a significant number of babies passionately loathe automobile travel, and will helpfully share this information with you by screaming at a pitch designed to encourage you to crash into a concrete pillar. They are perhaps not yet sophisticated enough to appreciate the consequences of inflicting severe psychological harm on someone at the wheel of a 4,000-pound high-speed weapon.

Most car haters take issue not with the motion, but with the sophisticated rat-trap we call the infant car seat. On the plus side, carphobia is much like colic: it's largely the domain of very small infants. The magical six-month milestone heralds so much, not least permission to transition to a forward-facing car seat, which many babies prefer.

# 730 NIGHTS OF CRAP SLEEP

You deserve sincere congratulations when your child's second birthday rolls around. Unless you've been gifted with a baby whose primary source of joy is doing what they're asked to do every day and staring at the insides of their eyelids for 20 out of 24 hours, it will have taken some extraordinarily hard work to reach this milestone. How should one mark this occasion?

At two years of age, your toddler will be happy with a cookie, a balloon and a peanut butter and jelly sandwich. There is no need for catered extravaganzas featuring chic pastel cupcakes, mobile petting zoos and string quartets. You'd be better off funnelling your spare funds into a commemorative tattoo featuring your child's cherubic visage and a banner reading "Lesson Learned."

Your authors are the parents of five children and one stepchild between them. The examples we use in this book may at times seem far-fetched, but most are in fact borne of our own experiences. Our children have eaten caterpillars, rhododendrons and their own excrement. Our breasts are quite wretched. We've flirted inappropriately with doctors and earnestly described our gallstones while they tried to have a nice night out with their wife (sorry, Dr. Gabe).

We are also personally acquainted with a family who hired a string quartet for their son's second birthday.

No doubt, similarly amusing, deranged and perplexing things will happen to you, as you traverse the psychedelic landscape of early parenthood. Best of luck!

# ABOUT THE AUTHORS

**Bunny Banyai** lives in the suburb of St. Kilda in Melbourne, Australia, with her two daughters, stepdaughter, and a partner more adept than most at pigtails and braids. Working as a copywriter has gifted her with the ability to write engagingly about life insurance, kitchen tiles, and steam cleaning. Bunny co-authored *Mini Me Melbourne* where she shares some of her favorite kid-friendly destinations.

**Madeleine Hamilton** is a part-time historian, part-time writer and full-time mother of Posy, Patience and Saul. She co-authored *Mini Me Melbourne* and is a regular contributor to www.kidspot.com.au. Madeleine and her family happily reside in the northern suburbs of Melbourne, Australia.

## Acknowledgements

*The publisher would like to acknowledge the following individuals and organizations:*

**Editorial manager**
Melissa Kayser

**Project manager**
Alison Proietto

**Editor**
Michelle Bennett

**Editorial Assistant**
Anna Collett

**U.S. Conversion**
Lesley Bruynesteyn

**Design**
Erika Budiman

**Layout**
Megan Ellis

**Pre-press**
Splitting Image

**Photography credits**
*Front cover:*
Toddler in diaper (©iStockphoto.com/tarinoel)

All other images are ©iStockphoto.com/popcic and ©iStockphoto.com/anttohoho

Explore Australia Publishing Pty. Ltd.
Ground Floor, Building 1, 658 Church Street, Richmond, VIC 3121

Explore Australia Publishing Pty. Ltd. is a division of Hardie Grant Publishing Pty. Ltd.

**hardie grant** publishing

This edition published in 2016

First published by Explore Australia Publishing Pty. Ltd., 2014

Form and design © Explore Australia Publishing Pty. Ltd., 2014

Concept and text © Bunny Banyai and Madeleine Hamilton, 2014

A Cataloguing-in-Publication entry is available from the catalogue of the National Library of Australia at www.nla.gov.au

ISBN-9781741175134

Printed and bound in China by 1010 Printing International Ltd.

www.exploreaustralia.net.au
Follow us on Twitter: @ExploreAus
Find us on Facebook: www.facebook.com/exploreaustralia